This book is to be returned on or before the date above.
It may be borrowed for a further period if not in demand.

# Erogenous Zones

## A play

## Frank Vickery

Samuel French — London
New York - Toronto - Hollywood

## EROGENOUS ZONES

First performed by the Sherman Theatre Company at the
Sherman Theatre, Cardiff, on 17th September 1992, with
the following cast of characters:

| | |
|---|---|
| **Lesley** | Kathryn Dimery |
| **Alison** | Erica Eirian |
| **Andrew** | Geraint Morgan |
| **Tom** | Brendan Charleson |
| **Michael** | Stuart Hulse |

Directed by Phil Clark
Designed by John Elvery
Lighting designed by Keith Hemming
Company Stage Manager Maggie Higgins

## COPYRIGHT INFORMATION

### (See also page ii)

# CHARACTERS

**Lesley**
**Alison**
**Andrew**
**Tom**
**Michael**

The action takes place in Lesley's kitchen, Alison's flat
and Michael's flat

# SYNOPSIS OF SCENES

ACT I, Scene 1  Friday night
ACT I, Scene 2  Later that night

ACT II  Saturday


Time—the present

Other plays by Frank Vickery
published by Samuel French Ltd

All's Fair
Breaking the String
Family Planning
A Night on the Tiles
One O'Clock from the House
Spanish Lies
Split Ends
Trivial Pursuits

*One Act Plays*
After I'm Gone
Green Favours
A Night Out

# ACT I
## Scene 1

*Lesley's kitchen, Alison's flat, Michael's flat. Friday night on a May bank holiday weekend*

*The set is in three areas. There is the kitchen of a semi-detached house on a modern estate and two flats in a large Victorian house: the living-room and bedroom of a ground-floor flat and, above all this, the living-room of an upstairs flat. L is the front door to the building. C there are four steps which lead to Michael's flat upstairs*

*When the* Curtain *rises, the stage is in darkness. Music begins (perhaps Queen singing "Somebody to Love")*

*During the first eight bars or so, the cast enter and take up their positions on stage. Andrew sits on the sofa in Michael's flat reading a holiday brochure. Lesley stands motionless in her kitchen with a suitcase in her left hand and her right hand outstretched placing a note to the front of the fridge. Alison sits on her bed with her arms wrapped tightly around Tom's waist. He stands very close to her with his hands up in the air away from her. There has been a struggle between them and, for the moment at least, they are frozen. Michael stands* c

*The music stops playing. A spot comes up on Michael. A very low soft light comes up on the set. After a moment Michael addresses the audience*

**Michael** Saturday night, bank holiday weekend. Michael Bennett. Thirty-one and unemployed. I live at 23b Pontcana Street. That's the flat upstairs. I've lived there for three years. Before that I was with my parents. I'd still be with them now if they hadn't realized my lifestyle and asked me to leave. Actually they threw me out. Oh, by the way, it's just as well to mention at this point that this (*he opens out his arms slightly*) is more or less the end of the play. Have a look round. (*He turns round to look at the three areas*)

*A soft light gently comes up on each area*

Take everything in. (*Facing the audience*) All will be revealed in two hours, I promise. There is a plane leaving the airport in (*checking his watch*)

three hours and I've got no idea at this point if I'm going to be on it or not. Oh, I've got my ticket bought and paid for but ... things haven't gone exactly as I'd hoped. Something's come up: I won't tell you what, you'll find out soon enough and I really don't know if he's gone without me. I've got a terrible feeling he has.

*Suddenly Abba sing "Take a Chance on Me". The music begins immediately and the Lights change from their previous state to flashing coloured circles which move all over the three acting areas*

*Lesley leaves her kitchen. She takes her suitcase and her note with her. Andrew places the brochure under the coffee table and leaves the living-room of the upstairs flat, and Tom and Alison leave the bedroom*

*Michael trots upstairs to his flat and switches on a small table lamp. The music stops immediately*

(*To the audience*) Friday night. (*He presses the button of his stereo cassette and some very nice relaxing opera music is heard, a female voice. He lounges on the sofa. After a moment he reaches for the brochure. Reading aloud*) "Barcelona, Spain's city of the sea. Barcelona is rich in medieval architecture especially amongst the narrow alleyways of the Gothic Quarter, where you will find the Cathedral of Santa Eulalia and the majestic courtyard of the Episcopal Palace. A short stroll from here you will find the succession of streets called *Ramblas* full of shops, cafés, restaurants and flower stalls. Down by the sea is the colourful Barceloneta quarter with its inexpensive fish restaurants and café bars and famous monument to Christopher Columbus. Two hundred and nineteen pounds for seven nights."

*The music stops*

(*To the audience*) I could just about manage that.

*There is the sound of running water*

Trouble is, I don't want to go by myself. God knows I've dropped enough hints. He's either deaf or he's just not interested. I suppose he's just not interested. I say he, I mean Andy. Or Andrew as he prefers to be called. He's my flatmate. He's in the shower at the moment. Can you hear the water? (*He listens*) Hear it?

*The water stops*

It's stopped now. (*After a slight pause*) I lost my job about four months ago. Things were tough for a while, so to help ease things financially I took in a lodger.

*Andrew enters* L. *He is wearing a suit and is carrying a sports bag*

I'd no sooner advertised when there was a ring at the door.

*Andrew rings the doorbell. The Lights change. Michael stands at the top of the stairs*

**Andrew** Hi. Michael Bennett?
**Michael** Yes.
**Andrew** Andrew Duggan. I've come about your ad.
**Michael** (*a little taken aback*) I only put it in this morning.
**Andrew** Have to act fast these days. Can I come in?
**Michael** Of course, yes. Sorry. (*He steps back to let Andrew inside*)
**Andrew** It hasn't gone, has it? You seemed a bit vague.
**Michael** No.
**Andrew** For a minute there I thought someone had beaten me to it.
**Michael** No, you're the first. I didn't expect a reply so soon.
**Andrew** (*looking around*) It's not bad, is it? (*He places the sports bag down on the floor just outside the bathroom*)
**Michael** It's only a one-bedroom flat. You do understand that?
**Andrew** (*moving behind the sofa*) So it's twin beds then, is it? (*He laughs*)
**Michael** Er no.

*They share a look*

I have the bedroom. You have the settee. It pulls out.
**Andrew** That's fair enough.
**Michael** If you take it I think it should only be for a month.

*Andrew looks at him*

Better see how things work out ... then we'll take it from there.
**Andrew** Oh it'll work out. I'm sure of it.
**Michael** Really.
**Andrew** Yeah. (*Turning to face him*) I've got this gut feeling, you know?

*They stare. Michael smiles*

When can I move in?
**Michael** We haven't talked terms.

**Andrew**  What are you asking?
**Michael**  Half the rent.
**Andrew**  Which is?
**Michael**  Sixty quid a week.
**Andrew**  That's all right.
**Michael**  And half the running costs: light, heat, telephone and so on.
**Andrew**  Meals?
**Michael**  Buy your own, cook your own.
**Andrew**  (*smiling*) Tomorrow then. I'll be around about ten. Shall we shake on it? I wouldn't like to be gazumped.
**Michael**  I wouldn't do that.

*They shake hands. Maybe Andrew holds on a little too long*

There's not a lot to see but I'd have a look round if I were you, before you finally commit yourself. (*Indicating*) Kitchen's through there, bathroom there, and that door is my room.
**Andrew**  I'll have a quick browse then, but there's no problem.

*Andrew goes off into the kitchen*

**Michael**  (*to the audience*) It was only supposed to be a month. He's been here three. I like him. He's all right but — I'm still not sure I did the right thing. We get on fine but he's a bit like Jekyll and Hyde. One day he's everything a room-mate should be — more, even — and the next he's completely indifferent to me.

*Andrew begins to sing in the shower, off*

If I thought he was using me I'd ask him to leave ... so I'd rather not think about it. His money helps — and I don't like living by myself. Maybe I'm using him.

*At this point Andrew comes into the living area having just that minute stepped out of the shower. His hair is damp and he is wearing a large white towel around his waist. He goes to his sports bag which is next to the door and takes out a can of anti-perspirant. He shows Michael what he is taking out of the bag and shakes it vigorously as he turns to go back into the bathroom — singing as he goes. "You wanna be in my gang my gang my gang — wanna be in my gang, wo ho ho ho"*

(*To the audience*) Handsome little bugger, isn't he? He's showered but he's not going out. I've just been to the fridge and he's stocked up. He's

bought a chicken, garlic and breadcrumbs — and I think it's Chicken Kiev.
He's even chilling a bottle of plonk.

**Andrew** (*off, shouting*) Mike?

**Michael** Yeah?

**Andrew** (*off*) Got any plans for tonight?

**Michael** Nothing special, no. (*To the audience*) Perhaps this would be a good
time to come straight out and ask him. The worst he can say is no. (*He reads
the brochure*)

*Alison comes on L. She is carrying a bag of groceries. She goes into her flat
and puts the groceries down near the table*

(*To the audience*) That's Alison. She's late tonight. (*He picks up a small
toffee hammer and taps on a pipe which leads directly to the flat below*)

*Alison hears this and taps her radiator in response then takes off her coat
and throws it on the bed and goes out. Tom walks into his kitchen, (the
modern one) carrying a pile of exercise books and a glass of milk which
he has half drunk. He sits at the table and begins to mark the books*

*During the following, Michael runs down the stairs and into Alison's flat*

*Lesley comes into the kitchen carrying a tray of tea things*

**Tom** How did she do?

**Lesley** She picked at it. (*She sees that Tom has left a considerable amount
too*) Have you finished?

*He nods*

I don't know why I bother. (*She takes his plate and empties it along with
the other one from the tray into a pedal bin*)

**Tom** I didn't see you eat anything?

**Lesley** I ate earlier.

*Michael is now in Alison's flat*

**Michael** (*calling*) Al?

**Alison** (*off*) I won't be a minute. Put the kettle on.

**Michael** You're late tonight.

*Michael goes off into the kitchen*

**Alison** (*off*) I had a meeting.

*Lesley is about to take Tom's glass of milk but he grabs it back almost without looking up*

**Tom**  I haven't finished that.

*Lesley begins to tidy things away*

     It's still off then, is it?

*She looks at him*

     My game of squash.
**Lesley**  I told you yesterday I was going to a cane party.
**Tom**  Sounds erotic. Why can't Rachel sit with Mother?
**Lesley**  I don't think it's fair to ask. She didn't do well in her "mocks".
     Apparently she has an enormous amount of work to do if she has any hope
     of passing the nine. At least that's what her mother says.
**Tom**  Couldn't she swot here? It would only be for an hour. You should be
     back by then, shouldn't you?
**Lesley**  (*raising her voice*) I'm out for the evening, Tom. Joanne has laid
     things on. They usually do at those sort of get-togethers.
**Tom**  What things?
**Lesley**  Drinks and that.
**Tom**  (*sighing*) Well, fair enough then. I was only checking. I didn't want to
     let Colin down unless I absolutely had to, that's all.
**Lesley**  Haven't you told him you can't make it?
**Tom**  Yes ... of course I have, yes. But I said I'd let him know if there were
     any last minute change of plan.
**Lesley**  (*snapping*) Ring him then! Play your bloody precious game of
     squash. Leave her on her own, it doesn't bother me — she's your mother
     not mine, remember.

*Lesley empties the washing machine during the next few lines*

*Alison enters*

**Alison**  I could murder a coffee.
**Michael**  (*off*) You've had a visitor.
**Alison**  Who?

     *Michael comes in from the kitchen*

**Michael**  Twice.

**Alison** Tom?

*He nods*

Did you speak to him?
**Michael** The second time.
**Alison** What did he say?
**Michael** I told him I didn't know where you were. There was no message.

*Lesley goes off out into the garden with the linen basket*

*Immediately she disappears Tom picks up the telephone and dials*

**Alison** (*after a slight pause*) I bet it's off. He called to cancel.
**Michael** He never said.
**Alison** It must be to call twice.
**Michael** He could ring and do that.
**Alison** Oh no he couldn't. He rang and cried off the last time. He wouldn't
   know how to tell me a second time on the telephone.

*Alison's telephone rings. She answers it. Michael hurries to stand next to her
in order to listen in. Alison speaks into the telephone immediately before Tom
has a chance to speak*

**Alison** }
**Michael** } (*together*) Hallo, Tom.

*Alison pushes Michael away slightly*

**Tom** (*quietly*) How did you know it was me?
**Alison** It wasn't difficult. Why are you whispering?
**Tom** I'm in the kitchen.
**Alison** What?
**Tom** (*a little louder*) Lesley's in the garden, I'm in the kitchen. I called to
   see you.
**Alison** Yes, I know.
**Tom** (*after a slight pause*) Listen, I may have to hang up quickly. When
   Lesley comes back I'll ——
**Alison** Yes yes, I understand. (*Slight pause*) Did you want something?
**Tom** It's difficult for me on the telephone.
**Alison** Then why did you ring?
**Tom** You weren't there when I called. (*Pause*) Umm ... it's about tonight.
**Alison** You're not coming. (*She looks at Michael*)

**Tom** I'm afraid not, no.

**Alison** (*determined*) I've planned a meal. Done all the shopping for it.

**Tom** I just can't get out of it, Al, honest. It's just that Lesley has this wicker and cane thing and someone has to stay with Mother.

**Alison** What about the kid next door? Gretchen?

**Tom** (*correcting her*) Rachel. Lesley doesn't think we should ask her.

**Alison** (*trying to tempt him*) Sod Lesley, I've got Chicken Kiev.

**Tom** Maybe I can swing something for tomorrow.

**Alison** If you don't turn up for this meal, Tom, there's only going to be one thing swinging tomorrow and that's you.

**Tom** Look, try and understand.

*A pause*

**Alison** This is not on, you know.

   *Lesley comes in from the garden*

*Tom hangs up*

**Michael** He's crying off?

**Alison** (*putting her hand over the receiver*) You wouldn't believe the excuse he's got. (*Back into the telephone*) Look, Tom ... Tom?

**Lesley** (*putting the empty linen basket on top of the washing machine*) There's a yoghurt in the fridge — take it to her. Maybe she'll eat that.

   *Lesley exits*

**Alison** (*to Michael*) He's hung up. Sixteen pounds I spent in that shop.

**Michael** Well you will go to Marks and Sparks, won't you, luv?

*They pause*

   *Meanwhile, Tom gets a yoghurt from the fridge and takes it to his mother*

**Alison** There's too much of it to waste ... What are you doing tonight? Do you fancy ——?

**Michael** I'd love to eat with you, Al, but Andrew's got something planned.

**Alison** For the two of you?

**Michael** Well I presume so. He wouldn't go to all that trouble just for himself.

**Alison** So it's just you and him then?

**Michael** Yeah, I think I might have cracked it at last.

**Alison** It's odd, isn't it? You want to get into a relationship, and I think I want to get out of mine.

**Michael** Oh yeah, that was obvious from the way you practically put a gun to his head to get him to come over.

**Alison** That's my point. I shouldn't have to do that.

**Michael** Who cares as long as he comes.

**Alison** I do. It never used to matter before but it does now. Why is that?

*He shrugs*

I'm getting older I suppose and some things just aren't good enough anymore. (*Slight pause*) You know something? I don't like my life very much.

**Michael** OK, so do something about it. Have you told Tom?

*She shakes her head*

Then tell him how you feel. Talk to him, you idiot.

**Alison** I hardly see him. That's part of the problem. Mind you, we don't talk much when we do see each other.

**Michael** (*smiling*) Oh?

**Alison** He's usually in such a knot when he gets here, all he wants to do is unwind.

**Michael** You mean undress.

**Alison** I mean both. (*Slight pause*) I don't know what I feel for him anymore. He still hurts ... and you can only be hurt by people you still care about, right?

*He smiles*

If he didn't mean anything then it wouldn't matter that we don't see each other that much ... so I suppose I do still care. I'm just not sure these days how much.

**Michael** Enough to commit yourself to him and you would.

**Alison** (*after a slight pause*) I'm not very happy.

*Michael stands behind Alison and puts his arms around her*

**Michael** Who is? You show me two happy people and I'll show you at least one liar.

**Alison** That's a bit cynical.

**Michael** It's true. It's very rare two people are happy at the same time. (*He sways her from left to right*) It oscillates.

**Alison** I don't want to be the other woman anymore.
**Michael** (*letting Alison go*) Look luv, take the knocks and enjoy the good
  bits for what they are.
**Alison** There aren't any good bits these days.
**Michael** You've got to keep bouncing back. You're getting a case of
  Mistressitis.

*Andrew comes out of the kitchen door. He is fully dressed now*

**Alison** (*jokingly*) So what can I take for it?
**Michael** A deep breath? It'll pass.
**Alison** And if it doesn't?

*They look at each other. He doesn't have an answer*

*Andrew taps on the radiator above then immediately goes back into the
kitchen*

**Michael** That's for me. (*He makes to leave*)
**Alison** Enjoy your meal.
**Michael** I will.

*Michael goes*

*Alison stares after him for a brief moment then goes off into the kitchen*

*When Michael gets into his flat Andrew obviously isn't there. Michael sits
down on the sofa*

*Lesley comes into her kitchen with an armfull of washing (bed sheets). She
is putting them into the washing machine when the telephone rings*

**Lesley** Hallo? ... (*Surprised*) Oh ... Joanne. (*She glances towards the kitchen
door*) No, nothing. I didn't expect you to ring that's all. ... A what? Wicker
and cane party. (*Under her breath*) I don't believe this. Er ... nothing, I was
talking to Tom. Well, I'm not very keen on those sorts of things. It's
difficult anyway ... Tom has arranged a game of squash and I know he can't
get out of it. ... That's all right, thanks for asking me anyway. Bye. (*She
hangs up and continues to busy herself with the washing machine*)

*Andrew comes from the kitchen*

**Andrew** Listen ... I've bought a couple of things. I'm going to cook a meal.

**Michael**  Yes, I saw the fridge.
**Andrew**  Wouldn't do me a favour and help me out?
**Michael**  Of course I will ... only go easy on the garlic.
**Andrew**  No — I was going to ask you to go out. A film or something.
**Michael**  Oh ... all right, yeah I don't mind.
**Andrew**  Are you sure?
**Michael**  No, what do you fancy?
**Andrew**  No, I'm not going out. I meant just you.
**Michael**  Hang on. You want me to go out while you stay in and cook me a meal?
**Andrew**  No — not cook you a meal. I've invited someone round.

*He sees Michael's reaction*

I know perhaps I should have asked first, but I didn't think you'd mind. You don't mind, do you?
**Michael**  You want me out of the way.
**Andrew**  Only for a couple of hours.
**Michael**  Christ, I had it all wrong.

*An awkward pause*

*Lesley goes out into the garden*

**Andrew**  Is it all right?
**Michael**  No it's not all right. This is my flat and if you want to screw in it you ask me first.
**Andrew**  Yeah, I know I should have, but I ——

*Michael storms off into his bedroom, slamming the door*

*There is a pause. Andrew ponders what to do. He looks at the telephone, then at Michael's bedroom door. He goes and taps on it*

Mike, this is stupid. (*Slight pause*) Look, I've arranged everything. It'll be embarrassing if I back out now. Please? Is it all right? (*Slight pause*) Just for tonight? (*Slight pause*) If you don't answer I'll take it that it's OK then. (*Slight pause*) Is it OK?
**Michael**  (*off*) Fuck off !
**Andrew**  What's the problem? If it's money I can lend you a couple of quid.

*Michael opens his door and comes out. He is furious*

**Michael** Lend? You want to lend me money to get out of your way?
**Andrew** Have it then. I'll give it. Keep it. (*Reaching for his wallet*) Is a fiver all right?
**Michael** And you'd expect me to take it too, wouldn't you?
**Andrew** Look, make it ten. Call in and have a Chinese on the way home.

*Michael looks at him incredulously before slamming the door again*

*Andrew stands there with his money in his hand. After a pause he puts it back into his wallet. He goes to the telephone and dials. The phone in Lesley's kitchen rings*

*Lesley and Tom rush into the kitchen: Lesley from the garden, Tom from the house. Lesley gets there first. Tom sits at the table and continues to mark his books*

**Lesley** Hallo?
**Andrew** It's me — Andrew.
**Lesley** I think you must have got the wrong number.
**Andrew** It is Lesley, isn't it ?
**Lesley** (*strained*) Yes.
**Andrew** Thank God for that. Look, something's come up. Tonight's off. I'll be in touch. (*He hangs up and goes to the sofa*)
**Lesley** (*into the telephone*) No, this is seven-three-eight-five-two-one. That's all right. (*She hangs up*)
**Tom** Who was that?
**Lesley** It wasn't anyone. A wrong number.
**Tom** (*looking up from his books*) Male or female?
**Lesley** (*after a slight pause*) Female. Why?

*Tom shrugs his shoulders and shakes his head. Slight pause*

Listen. Joanne rang just now. A few people have cried off and cancelled for tonight. You can play your game of squash.
**Tom** Can I.

*She nods. A slight pause*

Maybe I should stay in tonight.

*She looks at him*

Maybe we need a night in together.

**Lesley** Don't be silly — ring Colin.
**Tom** We can open a bottle of wine ... talk ... laugh.

*Tom puts his arm around her and pulls her towards him*

We haven't done that for a while.
**Lesley** (*pulling away*) We can do all that anyway. You go and have your
    game of squash and I'll chill a bottle in the fridge.
**Tom** (*after a slight pause*) Well ... if you're sure.
**Lesley** Ring him, go on.
**Tom** (*returning to his books*) There's plenty of time.
**Lesley** (*insisting*) You may as well do it now, otherwise he might have made
    other arrangements.

*A pause. He reluctantly goes to the telephone but dials Alison's number.
Lesley sits at the table with her back to Tom for the moment*

*Alison comes out of her bedroom to answer the telephone*

**Tom** Hallo Colin?
**Alison** Who?
**Tom** I can make it tonight after all.
**Alison** (*delighted*) Tom, it's you.
**Tom** That's right.
**Alison** You sound strange. Lesley's there.
**Tom** Of course.
**Alison** Right, I see. So it's back on then, is it?
**Tom** Lesley's arrangements have fallen through.
**Alison** Oh what a shame. What time shall I expect you?
**Tom** What time did you book the court?
**Alison** Seven-thirty?
**Tom** I'll see you there on the hour then.
**Alison** Bye.
**Tom** See you.

*They both hang up*

*Alison goes off into her kitchen*

*Tom smiles rather uncomfortably at Lesley*

I'd better go and spend half an hour with Mother.

*Tom leaves*

*Lesley stays in the kitchen*

   *Michael comes out of his bedroom*

*Andrew is sitting on the sofa reading the holiday brochure*

**Michael** (*to Andrew*) I've changed my mind.
**Andrew** What?
**Michael** You heard.
**Andrew** Why?
**Michael** I'm being silly and stupid. (*A slight pause*) No no don't try and tell me I'm not because I am. I will go out, but I won't take your money though.
**Andrew** I want you to.
**Michael** I couldn't.
**Andrew** Are you sure?
**Michael** Yeah.
**Andrew** OK then. Where will you go?
**Michael** Don't worry about it.
**Andrew** Will you see a film?
**Michael** Maybe.
**Andrew** Eleven o'clock should be all right.
**Michael** For what?
**Andrew** To come back.
**Michael** Eleven o'clock, right. (*Slight pause*) Thinking of going somewhere?

*Andrew looks up, not understanding what he means*

   The brochure.
**Andrew** Oh ... no. Well yeah. Spain perhaps. I've got a week coming. Don't fancy going by myself though.

*Michael looks up at the audience before going to tap on the radiator*

   *Tom comes back into the kitchen*

*Andrew goes to the telephone and dials. Michael goes downstairs to see Alison*

**Tom** (*to Lesley*) She's dropped off. Mother's dropped off.
**Lesley** (*sharply*) Wake her or she won't sleep tonight.
**Tom** She's only cat-napping.
**Lesley** (*insisting*) Wake her, Tom. It's not you who has to get up when she calls at three in the morning.

**Tom** Let her have an hour. She's exhausted.
**Lesley** I'm the one who's exhausted. (*Shouting*) Wake her!

*They stare at each other for a brief moment*

*Tom goes off to wake his mother*

*The telephone rings. Lesley answers it*

Hallo?
**Michael** (*going into Alison*) Alison, you'll never guess.
**Andrew** It's Andrew.

*Alison comes out of the kitchen*

**Alison** What?
**Lesley** Don't keep ringing.
**Michael** I am able to eat with you.
**Andrew** Can we talk?
**Alison** You are?
**Lesley** Make it quick.
**Michael** Is it all right?
**Andrew** It's back on for tonight.
**Alison** Well ...
**Lesley** What do you mean?
**Michael** It's not.
**Andrew** Change of plan — it's back on.
**Alison** Tom rang back. He's coming round.
**Lesley** (*desperately*) No it's not — it can't be.
**Michael** I see.
**Andrew** (*insisting*) Yes, I've managed to sort things out.
**Alison** What's happened with you?
**Lesley** (*can't believe it*) I can't come.
**Michael** (*making to leave*) Oh, I'll explain tomorrow.
**Andrew** Oh no, don't say that.
**Alison** Don't go — what's wrong? Isn't Andrew cooking?
**Lesley** When you called it off I told Tom he could play squash.
**Michael** Oh yeah, he's cooking ...
**Andrew** Tell him you've changed your mind.
**Alison** Then what's the problem?
**Lesley** I can't do that.
**Michael** It's not for me — it's for someone else.
**Andrew** Why not?

**Alison**  Oh Michael.
**Lesley**  He's made his arrangements.
**Michael**  I'll see you in the morning.
**Andrew**  Can't you come anyway?
**Alison**  No wait ...

*Michael is outside her flat now*

**Lesley**  I wish I could. I'm desperate to talk to you. There's Tom. (*She hangs up abruptly*) Shit!
**Alison**  Shit!
**Andrew**  (*hanging up*) Shit!
**Michael**  Shit!

*Black-out*

Scene 2

*The same. Later that evening*

*The Lights come up in Alison's flat and in Lesley's kitchen. Alison is sitting at the table facing the audience. Tom is putting his squash kit in his sports bag. He is wearing a short jacket*

**Tom**  (*to the audience*) Tom Medford. Thirty-four. School teacher. Married, no children, dying mother. She's very demanding and has never liked Lesley—that's my wife—from the start. She's lived with us now for four years and she still hasn't changed her mind about her. Lesley suffers her for my sake and for that I'm truly grateful although I rarely show it. (*Thinking about what he has said*) In fact I've never shown it. That often happens though, doesn't it? Often when you've been married for several years almost without realizing you start hiding things ... little insignificant things. Well I did anyway. You start off by lying, actually, but over a period of time you eventually progress to that. (*He has finished packing his bag and places it on the floor to his left. He sits at the table*)
**Alison**  (*to the audience*) Tom and I have known each other a long time. We were in teacher training college together. That's where we met. We were almost engaged once. We split up before we both qualified. After college I didn't see him for almost six years. I was having lunch out one Saturday and there he was ... two tables away.

*She looks over at Tom but he is not looking in her direction*

I recognized him immediately. Physically he hadn't changed at all. He kept looking over once or twice. (*Smiling*) I can see his face now. It took ages for the penny to finally drop.

*The Lights change: now only the two areas are lit in a tight circle. Music plays*

*Tom gets up as he recognizes Alison*

**Tom**  Alison?
**Alison**  (*getting up*) Hallo, Tom.
**Tom**  I wasn't sure. I'm sorry, I've been staring. May I?

*They walk nearer to each other until they are standing a few feet apart* c

How are you?
**Alison**  Fine.
**Tom**  Teaching?
**Alison**  Of course.
**Tom**  (*after a pause*)  Do you live near or what?
**Alison**  Ten minutes away by bus.
**Tom**  Still don't drive then?
**Alison**  I never went back to it, no.

*There is an awkward pause. Alison breaks it*

Well, it was very nice seeing you again, Tom.
**Tom**  Can we meet?
**Alison**  I don't think so. You're married.
**Tom**  Just for a drink and a chat.
**Alison**  Will you bring your wife?
**Tom**  If you'd like me to.
**Alison**  I would, yes.
**Tom**  You will then?

*She nods*

When?
**Alison**  (*immediately*) Wednesday.
**Tom**  Do you know the *Millers Arms*?
**Alison**  I'll find it.
**Tom**  There's a quiet lounge. Say about eight?
**Alison**  I'll look forward to seeing you ... both.

*Tom beams at her before he turns and exits L, taking his sports bag with him*

*The Lights change: only Alison's flat is lit*

(*To the audience*) I was early. I didn't plan it that way, in fact I would have preferred to have been a little late. Bang on eight o'clock he walked into the lounge ... alone. He fed me some cock and bull story about his wife not being able to make it. Half of me didn't really believe he would bring her and the other half was hoping he wouldn't. I made the customary effort to leave — he insisted on me staying for at least one drink and ten years later here we are. Older. Maybe a little wiser, certainly a lot more discontented. I'm speaking personally of course. We all change and ten years is a long time. I know I'm not the same person I was in those days and Tom certainly isn't. (*Slight pause*) He was never able to stay the night but we had some wonderful times together. I used to think he was mad. He was never very careful not to let things slip with Lesley. He was so irresponsible — but somehow that made it all the more exciting. He used to have me anywhere. I remember once, he had me here on this table. And just to add extra spice, he insisted on having the door open. He didn't really want to be seen — it was just the thought of the possibility of being caught. (*Slight pause*) Time is said to be a healer ... but sometimes I think it's got one hell of a lot to answer for.

*She goes into the kitchen*

*The Lights come up on Michael's flat*

*Andrew comes out of the bathroom wearing shorts and a vest. He is carrying a towel*

**Andrew** (*to the audience*) Great night this is turning out to be. Michael never came back after he went downstairs to see Alison, so I never had the chance to tell him that Lesley couldn't make it after all. I'm cooking the meal anyway, so he'll probably get some when he comes in. (*He begins to do press-ups on the floor*) I thought tonight was going to be perfect, and a damned sight cheaper than the hotels we've been using. Lesley's great though. She insists on paying half. I don't like to take it but it's OK to go Dutch these days. (*Slight pause*) I've never been with a married woman before. Anyone who has will know that it's different. The apple is always sweeter when it's stolen, right boys? OK so you're out with your wives tonight — but you know what I mean. Lesley is searching for something. I don't think she's going to find it in me, but I'm having a hell of a lot of fun helping her look. (*Slight pause*) Michael's searching too. I suppose we're all after something, that's what makes the world go round. And if I can make it go a bit faster for someone — (*he speeds up his press-ups*) — or a little slower — (*he slows them down*) — so what? All in a day's living, right? (*The telephone rings. He stops the press-ups and wipes his neck in the towel*) And you see, I've got this theory. (*Going to the telephone*) If you can help someone, and at the same time do a good turn for yourself — why waste your time being obstructive? (*Answering the telephone*) Hallo? ... Lesley. Where are you? ... Fantastic. Well, if you're at the bus station you get a twenty-five. Ask the driver to put you off at Cathedral Road. ... That's right. It's halfway down on the left. (*He remains on the telephone but continues his conversation in mime*)

*Alison comes out of the kitchen followed by Tom*

**Tom** Yes well there it is. (*Slight pause*) You haven't been listening to me.
**Alison** I have.
**Tom** I get the feeling you're not taking anything in. Somehow I don't seem to be getting through.
**Alison** Don't be silly.
**Tom** You're short with me. Ratty almost. You're not about to come on, are you?

*Alison sighs and makes a face*

See what I mean?
**Alison** What?
**Tom** You're aloof. Speaking's an effort. You make a fuss to get me here and all I've done since is listen to the sound of my own voice. All right, you have chipped in the odd word — given the occasional nod ——
**Alison** I wish I didn't have to do that.
**Tom** What?
**Alison** Make a fuss.
**Tom** It was awkward for me.
**Alison** But you're here. I've known you come when it was impossible.
**Tom** (*going to her and holding her to him*) The longer I know you the less I understand you.

*Andrew comes off the telephone and goes off into the bathroom*

*The Lights change: only Alison's flat is lit now*

**Alison** It always seems I have to fight to see you these days.
**Tom** I have to fight too.

**Alison**  Lesley?

**Tom**  Who else?

**Alison**  It's always the same.

**Tom**  And it always has been.

**Alison**  I remember a time — not so very long ago, when I used to win a lot more than I do now.

*Tom doesn't reply*

Who comes first with you, Tom?

**Tom**  I've had to skip a couple of nights and you feel threatened — that's what this is, isn't it?

**Alison**  I don't feel threatened at all.

**Tom**  What is it then?

**Alison**  I think I'm scared.

**Tom**  Of what?

**Alison**  I'm losing you and I'm scared because I think I want to. (*Annoyed with herself*) Oh why do I only think I want to?

**Tom**  Because you need reassuring.

**Alison**  I need more than that.

**Tom**  Proof then? Let me prove it to you.

*He kisses her; music plays: maybe "If You Don't Know Me By Now". They move into the bedroom and begin to undress each other, still kissing as they're doing it. Tom is down to his underpants and Alison to her bra and knickers. They get into bed and pull the covers over them. After a moment Alison's hand reaches up and switches off the light. The music stops at the same time as the Lights fade to Black-out. A spotlight comes up L*

*Lesley walks into it. She is wearing a light coat*

**Lesley**  (*to the audience*) I was nineteen and pregnant when I married Tom. We were married on December nineteenth and on January the eighth I miscarried. I used to think he'd have married me anyway in those days — but I don't suppose I'll ever know for sure. It was a good marriage once. Fourteen years is a long time to be with someone and I don't care who you are, people do drift in all kinds of directions. Oh, they might not have affairs ... but mentally I was beginning to leave Tom months before I met Andrew.

*Lesley exits*

*The spotlight fades. The Lights come up in Alison's bedroom. She and Tom are "at it". Tom's movements are energetic at first then he begins to slow down*

**Tom** (*absolutely exhausted*) Hurry up, for Christ's sake. (*He tries to continue*)
**Alison** It's no good — get off.

*He does*

**Tom** What happened?
**Alison** Nothing.
**Tom** That's what I mean. Why?
**Alison** (*ratty*) I don't know.
**Tom** We haven't done it for ages.
**Alison** You don't have to tell me.
**Tom** If you didn't feel like it you should have said.
**Alison** I did feel like it. I still feel like it.
**Tom** What's the problem then?
**Alison** Why are you asking me?
**Tom** (*getting out of bed, pulling up his underpants with his back to the audience*) I gave my all.
**Alison** You're saying it's my fault?
**Tom** It's your climax.
**Alison** You create it.
**Tom** You're blaming me? After all that effort you're blaming me?
**Alison** It shouldn't be an effort. Yours wasn't.
**Tom** No, and do you know why? It's because of the effort I put into it.
**Alison** So you're saying I didn't put anything into it?
**Tom** You were blocking me — it!

*Lesley comes on* L *dressed as before. She has a small piece of paper in her hand. She is looking for Andrew's address*

**Alison** (*shouting*) Oh I'm sorry. But it's just not possible for me to feel loved and assured and locked in ecstasy when you're shouting down my ear, "Hurry up, for Christ's sake".

*There is a ring at Alison's door. It is Lesley. Alison and Tom dress very quickly. As they are doing this, Lesley realizes she has rung the wrong bell. She presses the correct one and the Lights comes up in Michael's flat*

*Andrew comes out of the kitchen to answer the door*

**Andrew** I was beginning to think you were lost.

*Lesley goes into Michael's flat. The minute she disappears Alison is at her door. There is no-one there. She goes back inside*

**Tom** Who was it?
**Alison** It wasn't anyone. I'm going to check the chicken.

*Alison goes into the kitchen*

*Andrew and Lesley kiss passionately*

**Lesley** (*after a slight pause*) Something smells good.
**Andrew** Chicken. I hope you haven't eaten?
**Lesley** When you said you were cooking I didn't bother.
**Andrew** So you're hungry then?
**Lesley** Starved. Nice flat.
**Andrew** I was lucky to find it.
**Lesley** (*eyeing up the room*) Very cosy.

*A slight pause*

**Andrew** Plonk? Medium, sweet or dry. I wasn't sure which you'd like so I
  got one of each.
**Lesley** God knows how many times we've been out for a drink and you're
  still not sure what wine I like.
**Andrew** It's medium, isn't it?
**Lesley** It's dry.
**Andrew** Of course. I'll just get the glasses.

*Andrew goes off into the kitchen*

*Lesley slips off her coat and shoes and then sits in the armchair. Tom comes
out of the bedroom*

  *Alison comes out of the kitchen with two glasses and a bottle of wine. She
  places them on the table and pours*

**Tom** So you blame me because you didn't come.
**Alison** (*without looking at him*) Don't worry about it.
**Tom** But I do.
**Alison** Why? Has it happened before?
**Tom** I've never had any complaints.
**Alison** Neither have I.
**Tom** Stop this!
**Alison** What?
**Tom** We're playing games.
**Alison** No we're not. (*Slight pause*) It hurts, doesn't it? Knowing you didn't
  satisfy me?

*He doesn't answer. He sits in a chair at the table*

Ego bruised a little?

**Tom** Why didn't you fake it?

**Alison** You'd have preferred that?

**Tom** (*shouting*) Yes!

**Alison** Oh poor Tom. Why should I make it easy for you? Faking it isn't going to help us.

**Tom** And this is?

**Alison** I have faked it, Tom. For the last six or seven times I've faked it.

*She goes back into the kitchen*

(*As she goes*) Tonight I just wasn't up to it.

**Lesley** I don't know why ... but I imagined it to be bigger.

*Andrew comes in from the kitchen with the glasses and the wine*

**Andrew** What?

**Lesley** The flat.

**Andrew** Big enough for one. (*He pours the drinks*)

**Lesley** What is it — (*indicating the doors*) — bathroom and bedroom? (*She gets up to have a look*)

**Andrew** That's right. I'll give you a grand tour later.

**Lesley** (*opening the door to what she believes to be the bedroom*) Oh ...

**Andrew** That's the bathroom.

*She has a quick peep into the bedroom*

**Lesley** (*to Andrew*) A double bed?

**Andrew** I'm a restless sleeper.

**Lesley** It's not a bad size really.

*He hands her a glass of wine*

Two could be quite happy here. (*A slight pause*) You keep it very well. If I didn't know better I'd say it had a woman's touch.

**Andrew** (*smiling*) No no ... I do it all myself.

**Lesley** (*looking at her watch*) Can I use the telephone? I said I'd ring and check that everything is all right with Rachel — my dragon sitter.

*She picks up the telephone and rests it on the back of the sofa. She dials and while she is waiting for a reply she and Andrew kiss more. She has to break away when Rachel comes on the other end*

Hallo Rachel? ... Lesley. Everything all right? ... (*Firmly*) Wake her up. ...
No, don't let her sleep. ... Well talk to her — stick pins in her, anything, only
keep her awake. ... Yes, fine. I've just bought a beautiful wicker-basket. I
won't be late. Bye. (*She hangs up*) That woman gets more and more
nocturnal by the day. (*Laughing*) Or should I say by night.

**Andrew**  You told me she was on her last legs.

**Lesley**  Apparently she is. They only gave her eighteen months and that was
four years ago.

**Andrew**  (*getting up*) Listen. We've got a while yet. Still waiting for the
chicken. (*He gets the bottle of wine and his glass*) Do you want to have
another drink out here or shall we take the bottle in there? (*He bumps the
bedroom door with his bottom*)

*They both laugh then rush into the bedroom*

*Tom is still sitting — brooding*

*Alison comes out of the kitchen*

**Alison**  If anyone has the right to brood then it's me.

**Tom**  I'm not brooding.

**Alison**  What are you then?

**Tom**  Hungry.

**Alison**  You always are after sex.

*A slight pause*

**Tom**  Have you really faked it before?

*She smiles*

It's important to me that I satisfy you.

**Alison**  Is it?

**Tom**  Oh come on.

**Alison**  What about my other needs?

**Tom**  You're not satisfied?

**Alison**  Seeing you once in the last fortnight? No. Having a quickie one lunchtime the month before that — is not what I'm into. And it's not what you're
into either — or at least it never used to be. We're not seeing enough of each
other, Tom. If you want to satisfy me ——

**Tom**  I do love you ... you know that.

**Alison**  Then do something about it.

**Tom**  I have other responsibilities.

**Alison** (*raising her voice*) Your mother is going to live for years, Tom. She's outwitted every doctor in BUPA already. She'll see you in your grave, take it from me.

**Tom**  I can't leave while she's like she is.

**Alison**  What about Lesley?

**Tom** (*after a slight pause*) I don't want to hurt her.

**Alison** (*shouting*) Then what are you doing here? (*She answers herself*) Hurting me.

**Tom**  If I'm that much of a bastard why do you want me?

**Alison** (*turning to look at him*) For once I can't answer you.

**Tom**  I thought we were happy.

**Alison**  You show me two happy people and I'll show you at least one liar.

*A slight pause. Lesley comes out of the bedroom and sits on the floor at the coffee table*

It doesn't bother me that you still care for Lesley. I can handle that as long as I believe you care more for me. (*A slight pause*) There was a time when if I'd said that you'd have put your arms around me and told me that everything was going to be all right.

**Tom**  You haven't answered my question.

**Alison**  I've forgotten what it was.

**Tom**  No you haven't.

**Alison** (*determined*) Yes I've faked it a few times, yes. (*Going to the kitchen*) And I don't just mean the sex!

*Alison goes into the kitchen. Simultaneously Alison and Andrew come out of their kitchens carrying two dinner plates complete with meals plus a Goldspot spray. They place the plates on the tables*

**Andrew** (*announcing*) Chicken Kiev!

**Lesley**  God, I can't eat garlic.

**Alison**  Why not?

**Tom**  What will I tell Lesley?

**Andrew**  Don't worry — like a good boy scout, I'm all prepared.

*Andrew places the Goldspot on the table. So does Alison. Lesley and Tom pick it up immediately*

**Lesley**  What is it?

**Alison**  Goldspot.

**Andrew**  Guaranteed to leave your breath fresh and sparkling.

**Tom**  Are you sure about that?

**Andrew**  He'll suspect nothing, I promise.

*Both couples sit down and begin eating*

**Alison**  Wine?
**Lesley**  Not too much.

*They pour*

**Andrew**  Enough?
**Tom**  Fine.

*There is a pause while they eat*

**Alison**  Is it all right?
**Lesley**  Delicious. You'll make someone a lovely wife.
**Alison**  (*snapping*) Oh very bloody funny!
**Tom**  Sorry, sorry, bad joke. I shouldn't have said that.

*Pause*

**Alison**  Why are you rushing?
**Lesley**  I didn't realize I was.
**Andrew**  There's no need.
**Alison**  Take your time.
**Lesley**  I can't stay too long.
**Alison**  Why not?
**Tom**  A game of squash doesn't take all night.
**Alison**  By the time you shower — presumably have a few drinks with Colin.
**Tom**  If I leave at ten ... that should be all right.

*She gives him a long hard look before returning to her meal*

**Lesley**  Can I ask you a favour? (*Pointing to the basket beside the armchair*) That wicker waste-paper basket. Can I have it?
**Andrew**  (*amused at this request*) What?
**Lesley**  Will you give it to me?
**Andrew**  What do you want that for?
**Lesley**  I'm supposed to be at a wicker party. It will look a bit suspicious if I don't go home with anything.
**Andrew**  It's a bit awkward, actually.
**Lesley**  Isn't it yours?
**Andrew**  Oh yes it's mine. (*Trying to think of a good reason for not giving*

*it to her*) Only it was a gift from an aunt. When I moved in.
**Lesley**  Does she visit?
**Andrew**  (*awkwardly*) Not very often, no.
**Lesley**  Well she won't miss it then, will she?

*Andrew doesn't look very happy about it*

Please? I'll just feel a lot more comfortable going home with something.

*He looks at her for a brief moment then grabs her and pulls her down with him on to the sofa. More kissing*

*Tom and Alison have finished eating and are staring at each other*

**Tom**  (*after some time*) Say something.
**Alison**  There's no future for us is there, Tom?

*He can't answer*

I know we both knew that in the beginning, but neither of us cared then. You're not enough for me anymore. I want something permanent. I'd like to have it with you ... (*She trails off*) I'm thirty-six, I'm not unattractive. I'm still young enough to go shopping and old enough to count the change.
**Tom**  You're part of my life.
**Alison**  A very small part.
**Tom**  I need you. I need to come here whenever I can.
**Alison**  No, Tom. That's how it used to be. You even used to come here when you couldn't — and those were the best times. Remember? Now you come here when you think you should — and not always then.
**Tom**  That's not true.
**Alison**  But it is. And it's not good enough anymore.
**Tom**  (*after a slight pause*) You're saying you want to finish it?
**Alison**  I'm saying it's up to you. It's time to decide, Tom. You're going to have to make a choice.

*An uncomfortable continuous sound begins, starting quite low but growing in pitch. As it reaches a peak it stops quite abruptly. Immediately it stops, Lesley and Andrew part physically*

**Andrew**  (*unable to believe his ears*) What?
**Lesley**  I'm pregnant.

*A slight pause. Andrew gets up from the sofa*

**Andrew** What are you going to do?

**Lesley** What do you want me to do? It's yours.

**Andrew** Don't think I'm trying to get out of this but how do you know it's mine?

**Lesley** Because I haven't had sex with Tom for the past six months. We've been seeing each other for three and I think I'm two months gone.

**Andrew** Think?

**Lesley** I've missed a month. That's something I've never done.

**Andrew** It's not official then? I mean you haven't had a test or anything?

**Lesley** I'm pregnant, Andrew. You can put money on it. (*Slight pause*) I wasn't going to tell you until I'd seen a doctor ... but tonight seemed the right time.

**Andrew** (*frantically thinking what to do*) I'll give you money.

*She looks at him*

You don't want to keep it? The kid, do you?

*She starts to cry and empties her handbag on to the sofa in order to find her handkerchief. She has her back to Andrew. We don't hear her cry but we see her wipe her eyes*

Look ... um ... well it's the only thing to do, isn't it?

**Lesley** (*not really agreeing*) Of course.

**Andrew** I'll pay. I'll pay for it all.

**Lesley** I thought maybe you'd want it.

**Andrew** Keep the baby you mean?

**Lesley** I would if you would.

**Andrew** (*after a slight pause*) That would mean you'd have to leave Tom.

**Lesley** (*raising her voice a little*) Well he'd hardly want me with someone else's child. (*A slight pause*) You don't want me to leave him?

**Andrew** (*after a slight pause*) Er ... no. I don't, no. (*Slight pause*) Look, it's difficult not to appear the rat here but ... we have a good thing going, right?

*She doesn't answer*

Why spoil it all? No commitments — that's what we said, wasn't it? All right, we've got a problem but nothing that can't be sorted.

**Lesley** What am I going to tell Tom when I disappear for a few days?

**Andrew** You could be visiting someone.

**Lesley** Who?

**Andrew** (*screaming*) Anyone! (*A pause*) Don't you know anyone?

**Lesley** Please. Stick by me on this?

*Andrew goes to Lesley and holds her*

**Andrew** Of course I will. (*Turning her to face him*) It's our problem, right?
We'll sort it out. Then everything will be as before. I promise.

**Lesley** (*after a slight pause*) I've got to ask you this. I know you've never
told me, not once, ever ... but now I really need to know. (*Slight pause*) Do
you love me?

**Andrew** (*after a slight pause*) I don't think I've ever loved anyone.

**Lesley** (*swallowing hard*) I see.

**Andrew** I love being with you. I love going to bed with you ... (*Slight pause*)
But I'm not in love with you.

*Lesley looks at him*

Would you rather I lied?

**Lesley** (*shouting*) At this moment — yes! I think so.

**Andrew** It would only make you feel better until you asked me again. I
wouldn't have lied twice.

**Lesley** If we lived together you might ——

**Andrew** It wouldn't work.

**Lesley** You don't know till you give it a try.

**Andrew** Where would we live?

**Lesley** Here. It's big enough.

**Andrew** No.

**Lesley** If it worked out we could always look for something bigger——

**Andrew** (*shouting*) Lesley don't!

**Lesley** When I divorce Tom I'll get half. We'll be able to buy something——

**Andrew** (*shouting*) Don't! Don't do this to yourself. (*Pause*) Look, when
we've solved our problem, when things are back to normal, I want to go
on as we were. Good times — no commitments. You wanted that as much
as I did. Nothing's changed.

**Lesley** Except I'm pregnant.

**Andrew** That shouldn't make any difference.

**Lesley** But it does!

**Andrew** Only until you do something about it. Oh Les ... you feel vulnerable
now, but it'll pass. (*Slight pause*) Shall I tell you something?

*She looks at him*

You've never told me you love me either.

**Lesley** But I've wanted to. You haven't.

*Lesley goes off into the bedroom*

*Alison is now facing away from Tom downstage. Tom is facing front*

**Tom**  I'm sorry.
**Alison**  I promised myself I'd never ask you to choose between Lesley and
  me. I always knew I'd get the short straw.
**Andrew**  (*calling into the bedroom*) Are you sure you're all right?
**Lesley**  (*off*) Yes.
**Andrew**  I'd rather walk you some of the way.

*Lesley comes out of the bedroom*

**Lesley**  No, I'll be fine. (*She puts on her shoes*)

*Pause*

**Andrew**  I'll be in touch then?

*She nods hesitantly*

  Ring me.
**Lesley**  No. You ring me.

*There is another awkward moment when they are both not sure whether to
kiss. It becomes obvious it's not going to happen. Lesley turns to get her bag
from the sofa. Andrew remembers the wicker basket and bends to pick it up.
By the time Lesley turns to face him he is holding it out towards her. She
almost snatches it from him. She makes to leave, taking her coat*

**Andrew**  Wait. (*He picks up the Goldspot and throws it into the basket*)

*She is halfway down the stairs*

  (*Calling after her*) See you.

*Lesley stops for a moment. She takes the Goldspot from the basket, sprays
it into her mouth once or twice, then walks off L*

*Andrew hovers for a moment before going off into the kitchen*

*Alison is sitting at the table. Tom is standing behind her*

**Tom**  I don't know what else to say. (*He puts his hands on her shoulders*)
**Alison**  (*shrugging him away*) No don't.

**Tom** Why spoil it by wanting more?
**Alison** (*holding up the Goldspot*) Go away, Tom.

*Pause. Tom takes his coat from the back of the chair then takes the Goldspot from Alison. He leaves. Outside her flat he pauses before spraying the Goldspot into his mouth. Having done this he storms off* L

*Alison is obviously upset. She gets up from the table and in a fit of frustration sweeps everything off it before tipping it up on its side. She then goes off into her bathroom*

*Andrew comes on from the kitchen with wine. He drinks it straight from the bottle. He lays down on the sofa, drinks and eventually goes to sleep*

*Lesley, still carrying the wicker basket, enters her kitchen and switches on the light. She puts down the basket and grabs a quiet moment to herself*

*A door slams*

**Lesley** (*calling*) Tom? (*She busies herself*)

*Tom comes in wearing his coat and carrying his sports bag*

How did it go?

*He looks at her*

The squash?
**Tom** Oh, fine. Fine. (*He starts emptying his bag on to the table*) Mother all right?
**Lesley** She's watching *Newsnight*.
**Tom** Been all right then, has she?
**Lesley** As far as I know. Joanne rang back after you left. The wicker party was all back on. I told her it was difficult for me but you know Jo. I asked Rachel to come in. (*She has a sneaky squirt of Goldspot*)
**Tom** Well that's rich. You didn't think she should be asked to sit for me.
**Lesley** It was for Joanne. You know how neurotic she is. If I hadn't gone I think that she would have had a nervous breakdown. (*She takes the clean sheets from the washing machine*)
**Tom** Mother had her Horlicks? (*He has a sneaky squirt of Goldspot*)
**Lesley** Ten minutes ago. (*Slight pause*) Er ... listen. I've been thinking. Holiday. We haven't had one since God knows when, why don't we make arrangements for Mother and go off somewhere. Spain or something.

**Tom**  What's brought all this on?

**Lesley**  Nothing. (*Slight pause*) Well it was Jo, actually. Something she said. What do you think? Is it a good idea?

*No answer*

I think it would be good for the two of us to get away — spend some time on our own. (*Slight pause*) Well, shall I arrange something? (*Quickly*) Why are you looking at me like that.

**Tom**  Is there anything wrong?

**Lesley**  Wrong? (*She puts Tom's squash clothes into the washing machine*)

**Tom**  It's all so out of the blue. What was it exactly Joanne said?

**Lesley**  I just fancy the idea of spending some time away, that's all ... fancy spending some time together. (*Slight pause*) Fancy spending some time together?

*No answer*

Look — I know things have been a bit strained between us this last couple of months ... well they haven't been right, anyway. The truth is neither of us have been very happy.

**Tom**  You show me two happy people and I'll show you at least one liar.

**Lesley**  A short break together would do us the world of good. Clear the air. Recharge the batteries.

*Pause as they look at each other*

What do you say?

*He doesn't say anything. He half smiles and nods ever so slightly*

Good. Perhaps you can call into the travel agents tomorrow and see what's available.

**Tom**  But you can do that, can't you?

*She looks very uncomfortable. She half nods. She picks up the linen basket of clean washing and is about to take it out into the garden*

Will you sit with Mother for quarter of an hour? (*He goes to the door*) I'm going to have a shower.

**Lesley**  Didn't you shower at the centre?

*Tom is caught briefly for an answer*

**Tom** They weren't working. Can you believe that?

*Tom half turns to leave. Lesley does the same. Both sneak one last spray of Goldspot before going off*

*Alison comes out of her bathroom. She is wearing pyjamas. She is still upset. She looks at the mess in the living area before going into her bedroom. She sits on the bed*

*Michael enters L*

*As he passes Alison's flat he stops briefly and thinks about knocking but changes his mind. He goes up into his flat. He sees Andrew fast asleep on the sofa. He goes to him and shakes him gently. Andrew mumbles but doesn't wake*

**Michael** I'm back.

*Andrew stirs again*

You haven't made up your bed.

*Alison gets under her duvet*

**Michael** The settee — you haven't pulled it out. You haven't made your bed.
**Andrew** (*still very groggy*) It's all right ... it's all right. Don't worry about it.
**Michael** Shall I give you a hand?
**Andrew** I'm too tired. I can't be bothered.

*Music starts to play: maybe "I'm Not In Love"*

*At this point Tom comes into his kitchen wearing his dressing-gown. During the following he looks in a cupboard for a bottle of shampoo. He finds it and leaves*

**Michael** Do you want to come in with me?

*No reply*

Andrew?

*Still no answer*

You can share with me if you ...

*He realizes it's hopeless. He takes off his short jacket; for a moment we think he might be joining Andrew on the sofa, but he places the jacket over him*

*Dejected, Michael goes to his bedroom, putting the light out as he goes*

*Keeping the same position on her bed, Alison stretches up and switches off her light*

*As Tom leaves the kitchen he does the same*

*Black-out*

CURTAIN

# ACT II

*The same. The following morning: Saturday 9.15 a.m.*

*Tom's kitchen is brightly lit giving the impression of a sunny day. There are no breakfast things about so it looks as if they've been up for some time — although no-one is around. Alison is still asleep. We see her form under the duvet in her darkened room. Her living area has some light. She didn't conpletely close the curtains the night before and there is a shaft of sunlight through the gap. The room is exactly as she left it, with all the remains of the dinner still on the table and floor. Michael's flat doesn't look very tidy either. Things have not been cleared away. Andrew is not on the sofa — the room is empty*

*After a moment Michael comes out of his bedroom. He has not dressed. He is wearing just a dressing-gown and underpants. He looks at the mess, then at the sofa, then back at the mess*

**Michael**  I shouldn't have to clean up this mess. Do you have any idea what you're doing to me? (*Putting the empty bottles and glasses on a tray*) You show me no respect. But do you know what hurts most? I let you treat me like that. I let you because I'd rather be hurt by you than ignored by you. The thing is — most of the time I'm both by you. It doesn't make sense. I should leave all this for him. It's Saturday, he's got a half-day but I can't bear to look at it until twelve o'clock.

*Michael carries the tray off into the kitchen*

*A small coloured light comes up in Alison's living area for the dream sequence*

*Tom briskly walks on L. He goes straight into Alison's flat and stands in the middle of the living area*

**Tom**  (*calling out*) Can I come in?

*Alison stirs slightly*

I came over to talk.

**Alison**  I thought we said it all.

**Tom**  I've changed my mind. I made a mistake. You put me on the spot and I made a mistake. I want you.

**Alison**  I don't want an affair, Tom.

**Tom**  I know. I understand that. I haven't come back to ask you to go on as before. Things have come to a head, I realize that. Walking home last night and lying awake in bed I had time to think — about you — about me, and Lesley. For years I've dreaded the time when you'd ask me to leave Lesley. I knew if we were together long enough it would come up and sure enough last night there it was. I panicked. I panicked and made a wrong decision. I made a mistake and I'm asking you to let me put it right.

**Alison**  How?

**Tom**  By leaving.

**Alison**  Lesley?

**Tom**  Of course.

*She smiles briefly into the pillow before looking up again*

**Alison**  Tom, I've been thinking a lot too.

**Tom**  Come on, don't let's play games. I've put my cards on the table. Just answer me one simple question. Do you want me or not?

**Alison**  (*quickly*) Yes.

*She kneels on the bed. Tom rushes into her*

Yes yes yes yes yes!

*They embrace*

When will you leave?

**Tom**  A week? Next Wednesday? Today if you like.

**Alison**  What about your mother?

**Tom**  Yes, I'll have to sort something out there, won't I?

**Alison**  What exactly?

**Tom**  I don't know. Sheltered accommodation, something like that I suppose. I don't want you worrying about it. I'm going to take care of everything.

*They kiss a few times*

Do you know what I fancy right now?

*She tries to drag him down on the bed but he resists*

No ... no, listen. A coffee.

**Alison**  How boring.

**Tom**  A really strong cup of coffee.

**Alison**  Well you know where the kitchen is.

**Tom**  I thought maybe you'd like to do it for me.

**Alison**  (*affectionately*) Did you now. You move in here all those sort of things are shared.

**Tom**  Really?

**Alison**  Well I might let you off once in a while.

**Tom**  Shall I start by putting the kettle on?

*Suddenly Tom picks her up in his arms*

**Alison**  Tom, what are you doing? Put me down.

**Tom**  Since I'm not going to get the opportunity to carry you over the threshold for some time — I thought I'd carry you into the kitchen instead.

**Alison**  (*very happy*) Oh Tom, it's not going to go wrong, is it? Lesley could make it difficult for us.

**Tom**  I don't want you worrying about Lesley.

**Alison**  What if she won't give you up?

**Tom**  Yes, I've thought of that and the only thing I can come up with is that you move out of this place — we'll sell the house, and the four of us will live together in a nice big semi somewhere !

*She screams at the thought. Tom runs off with her into the kitchen*

*Immediately they are off, Alison screams again and her double (dressed in an identical wig and pyjamas) sits up in bed and puts her hands to her face. She gets out of bed and runs into the bathroom*

*The dream sequence ends and the Lights revert to their previous state*

   *Lesley comes into her kitchen*

*She goes to the sink and picks up a dishcloth and proceeds to wipe down the kitchen table. As she is doing this the telephone rings. She is about to answer it when it stops. She ponders for a moment, thinking it might be Andrew. Hesitantly she picks up the phone and dials. Michael's telephone rings*

   *He comes out of his bedroom to answer it. He is properly dressed this time*

**Michael**  Hallo?

**Lesley**  Andrew?

**Michael**  No, he's at work. (*Slight pause*) Who is this?

*She hangs up. Michael thinks this strange. While tidying the sofa cushions he finds a bunch of keys. He stands and looks at them. There is a key tab on the ring with the owner's name and address. Michael reads it*

*He makes a decision and runs off into the bedroom*

*Lesley is standing motionless at the table*

**Lesley** *(to the audience)* I worked all my married life up until a few years ago when I stopped to take care of Tom's mother. Three months of her and I was screaming to go back to work. Tom wouldn't hear of it, it would have meant putting his mother into care. But he compromised eventually and I found a part-time job. Going home one lunchtime, one of the girls wanted to book a holiday and she asked if I'd come to the travel agents with her. While she was being seen to I browsed through a few brochures. Towards the back of the office there was a rather large desk.

*Music: "Cavatina". The Lights change*

Someone was sitting at it frantically tapping information into a desk computer. Suddenly the telephone rang and he looked up to answer it. We caught each other's eye. He was beautiful. I found myself asking all sorts of questions about a holiday I had no intention of buying. I left my number with him under the pretence of him finding me a more suitable holiday. I waited almost a fortnight for him to ring. He never did. I took to walking home that way from work hoping to bump into him. I shocked myself. I couldn't believe I was behaving in that way. Before the day I walked into his office I was a reasonably unhappy, married woman. Now I started dreaming about him. I'd never seen anyone in my life that I wanted so much. I felt I was being driven by some incredible force. I was quietly becoming obsessed. Almost without thinking I was back in his office again, telling him a pack of lies. I was ashamed of the way I was acting but my feelings were so strong I just couldn't help myself. Eventually, he did ring me at home. Tom was out at the time, thank God — and the rest is history. *(Slight pause)* I don't know to this day why I did it — why I allowed myself to do it. All I know is, from the moment he looked at me, he saw something ... some ... *(She searches for the word)* Some corner of my soul, that until then I didn't know existed. No-one I've known has ever been able to do that.

*The Lights change. Pause*

I don't know what's going to happen to me now, but all I can say is — although I made everything happen — I feel my behaviour was ... is, alien

to me — and that I ... me — Lesley Medford — had very little or nothing
to do with it.

*She goes off into another part of the house*

*Michael comes out of his bedroom. He is wearing a rather short, distinctive blouson-type jacket. He has made up his mind to return the keys. He leaves his flat, running down the stairs and goes straight into Alison's. Just before Michael has entered her flat she comes out of her bathroom, (she has dressed by this time) and in a temper tips over the chairs in the messed-up living area. Michael comes in*

**Michael** Jesus. Did you do this?
**Alison** (*shouting*) Who else lives here!

*He tries to clear up*

No, don't — leave it. I'll do it later.
**Michael** You want to talk about it?
**Alison** No!
**Michael** Yes you do.
**Alison** You know what it's about.
**Michael** Tom.

*She nods*

Don't tell me he didn't turn up?
**Alison** Oh he turned up.
**Michael** (*after a slight pause*) And?
**Alison** One thing led to another.
**Michael** Obviously.
**Alison** I just couldn't let it go on anymore.
**Michael** You finished it.
**Alison** I made him choose.
**Michael** Oh shit!
**Alison** I didn't think he could hurt me anymore.
**Michael** (*thinking what to do*) Coffee.
**Alison** No! You think you're strong — you think you're on top — and although I've known for years he wouldn't choose me, I can't tell you how I felt when I heard him say it.
**Michael** Whisky.
**Alison** Shall I tell you what I need more than anything now? Company. I don't want to be on my own.

**Michael** Do you want him back?

**Alison** It wouldn't be the same.

**Michael** It might even be better.

**Alison** He wouldn't come back — it's over.

**Michael** Has he given back his key?

**Alison** No.

**Michael** Then it's not over. Believe me it's never over till they hand in their key. (*Slight pause*) I'm sure you can patch all this up.

**Alison** Part of me wants to — and part of me wants to turn away. World War Three is going on inside me and all I really want to be is a conscientious objector.

**Michael** What you really want is to win.

**Alison** What can I do?

**Michael** Fight. If I wanted someone that much, I'm damned if I'd give him up that easily. Do you really want him?

*No answer*

You've got to know what you want before you go after it.

**Alison** I don't want to go after anything ; or anyone who doesn't want to be got!

**Michael** Alison, make him want it.

**Alison** If I knew how to do that he'd have chosen me and not Lesley.

**Michael** Lesley?

**Alison** His wife.

**Michael** (*almost laughing*) It's ironic how much we have in common. That cosy little meal and bottle of plonk last night was for Andrew and a fella called Lesley.

**Alison** What?

**Michael** I found the keys, didn't I. There's a tag with his name and address. Against my better judgement, I thought I'd return them. Fancy a ride on the bus?

**Alison** I don't think you should.

**Michael** I know but I want to. I want to see the opposition.

**Alison** It's a bad idea.

**Michael** Haven't you ever seen Tom's wife?

**Alison** No, never.

**Michael** Well I've made up my mind. Are you coming?

**Alison** I think I'd better stay and clear up this lot.

**Michael** I'll see you later then. I won't be long. I'll call in when I get back ... let you know how I got on. (*He goes*)

**Alison** (*calling*) Just don't come back with a black eye.

*Michael exits* L

*Alison starts to clear up her living area*

*Lesley comes into the kitchen followed by Tom. He has his coat on and is about to leave*

*Lesley takes the clean bedding out of the washing machine and puts it on the table. Throughout the following scene she folds the bedding*

**Tom** Well, shall I or shan't I?

**Lesley** (*indifferent*) It's up to you.

**Tom** I know I said for you to call in and pick some up, but it's nothing for me to do it on my way back.

**Lesley** Do it then.

**Tom** Why do I feel it's not what you want?

**Lesley** It doesn't matter to me one way or the other.

**Tom** Then you call in. You do it.

**Lesley** If you like.

**Tom** Look, what is it with you?

**Lesley** Tom — if you want to call in and pick up some brochures, call in — if you don't — I'll do it.

**Tom** Why do I get the impression you'd rather me not go there.

**Lesley** (*impatiently*) Tom!

**Tom** You've changed your mind, is that it?

**Lesley** (*deliberately*) I have not changed my mind!

**Tom** Then what's the matter with you this morning? There's something wrong. You're different.

**Lesley** Don't be ridiculous. I'm just busy, that's all. Your mother hasn't given me five minutes this morning.

**Tom** Oh no — you can't blame her — not this time. You're completely different to how you were last night. I wish I knew what it was.

**Lesley** I wish you'd get out of my way. Go if you're going.

**Tom** Have I said something?

*No reply*

If it's me — tell me.

**Lesley** (*quietly*) It's not you.

**Tom** What is it then?

*Pause*

**Lesley**  This holiday. A good idea but the timing is all wrong.
**Tom**  So you don't want to go?

*She stops folding a blanket and stands with her back towards Tom*

**Lesley**  I need a break, Tom ... but I need a break from everything. (*Slight pause*) You included. Oh I don't mean a fortnight in Spain ... just a weekend perhaps. Somewhere quiet where I can relax and be alone. I need that more than I need anything.
**Tom**  That's it. I knew there was something. You haven't looked at me once this morning. Look at me.

*She continues to fold the blanket*

Come on look at me. (*Shouting*) Look at me!

*She immediately turns and they stare at each other for a moment*

We're in trouble.

*Repeat the same sound effect from Act I*

*A second or two after it begins, Andrew appears* L

*He crosses and goes straight up into the flat. All the time the sound is increasing in pitch*

**Andrew**  (*calling*) Mike?

*He looks in at Michael's bedroom and then does the same at the kitchen door but Michael is nowhere to be seen. As Andrew shuts the kitchen door the sound effect stops*

Shit! (*He takes two airline tickets from his pocket and puts them on the coffee table*)

*Tom goes off leaving Lesley alone in the kitchen. Andrew goes into the bathroom*

*Alison is standing behind her table. Lesley similarly. Throughout the following scene, Lesley folds the bedding and puts it into the linen basket, and Alison resets her furniture and makes her bed*

**Lesley** (*to the audience*) My mother used to say that you could always tell if your husband is messing around by the number of times he changes his underwear. There was no advice to the man on the woman. (*Slight pause*) I wonder if I've left any tell-tale signs.

**Alison** (*to the audience*) My father changed his underclothes twice a week every week for his entire married life. He was married for thirty-six years — "carried on" for twelve and my mother didn't know a thing. Maybe it's the same with Lesley.

**Lesley** The biggest give-away, I think, is "mood".

**Alison** I don't think I could hide mine from my partner ... well, not successfully, anyway.

**Lesley** It's not easy to deceive — but like everything, the more you do it, the easier it gets.

**Alison** I'm not against a little fibbing. A little lie here and there never did anyone any harm — and sometimes saves a lot of pain.

**Lesley** I hate it. I do it because I have to — but I hate it.

**Alison** But then of course it snowballs, doesn't it? You start off by lying about where you're going — then you lie about who you were going with, then what you were doing and where you were doing — it, so pretty soon you're not only lying to your partner, you start lying to yourself as well because you actually start to believe the lie — and that's where it starts to get dangerous.

**Lesley** Everything should work out OK providing you keep it in check. The trouble is of course, once you're caught in this tender trap, common sense and reason go out of the window. And it's not as if you have any warning. No signals as to what's going to happen. There's no knock on the door so you don't have the opportunity of not answering.

**Alison** Or shutting him out. You're not even aware that he's got one foot over the threshold.

**Lesley** Just suddenly — he's there.

**Alison** Standing in the middle of this space inside you.

**Lesley** You don't know how he got there ——

**Alison** And by that time you don't care ——

**Lesley** Something tells you you ought to be frightened ——

**Alison** Because you feel violated in some way ——

**Lesley** But you feel too wonderful to feel threatened.

**Alison** And yet the whole business makes you completely and utterly vulnerable.

**Lesley** (*after a slight pause*) And that's kind of scary.

*Andrew comes out of the bathroom and dials Alison's number*

**Alison** I wonder if she knows. Some women do and ignore it. Some find out and go to pieces. I wonder what Lesley would do. (*Her telephone rings*)

*Lesley takes the washing out into the garden*

(*Into the telephone*) Hallo?

**Andrew** It's Andrew. I don't suppose Michael's there?

**Alison** No, he's not.

**Andrew** Any idea where he is?

**Alison** I'm afraid not, no.

**Andrew** So you wouldn't know if he's due back or anything?

**Alison** Er ... no.

**Andrew** Right. OK. Er ... listen — when he does come back, if he should pop in to see you first, will you tell him I want to see him?

**Alison** Yes I will.

**Andrew** It's urgent. Bye.

**Alison** Bye.

*They both hang up*

*Alison goes into her kitchen. Andrew goes into the bathroom. Michael enters* L

**Michael** (*immediately to the audience*) See? I said I wouldn't be long, didn't I? Alison's never going to believe me when I tell her. (*He makes for Alison's flat*) I'm not sure she'll want to believe it. I mean at this stage in her emotional crisis, I don't know whether it's good news or not. (*He steps into her flat*) That's better. At least it looks like a living-room now.

*Alison comes out of the kitchen carrying a plate of fried scampi*

I'm glad to see that the whole business hasn't put you off your food.

**Alison** This is the first thing I've eaten all day.

**Michael** (*taking a scampi*) Boy, have I got news for you!

**Alison** There's more in the kitchen if you want some. Go and help yourself.

*He does. He takes his coat off and leaves it on the back of the chair before going*

(*Calling after him*) They're in the freezer but the fat's still hot.

**Michael** (*off*) This news: you'd better sit down.

**Alison** Oh by the way, Andrew just rang.

**Michael** (*off*) Are you sitting?

**Alison** Did you hear what I said? He was looking for you. Wants to see you straight away.

*Michael puts his head around the kitchen door*

**Michael** Straight away?

**Alison** (*sitting at the table*) Urgent, he said.

**Michael** Well he's just going to have to wait, isn't he? Good, you're sitting. Are you comfortable?

**Alison** Just get on with it.

**Michael** Well, bombshell number one. I found the address on the keytab with extreme difficulty. I had to change buses and when I finally got there no-one had heard of the address.

**Alison** I hope you're not letting that fat burn.

*Michael rushes off back into the kitchen*

**Michael** (*off*) I eventually found it and rang the doorbell.

*Lesley's doorbell rings*

(*Off*) Now I expected some sort of Adonis to be standing the other side of the door, but this piece about thirty-five answered. She didn't look anything special. Where's the master of the house, I asked myself, he's the one I've come to feast my eyes on. Anyway, I explained about the keys and she asked me in.

**Alison** Oh will you please get on with it.

**Lesley** (*off*) No, please — it's the least I can do.

*Lesley enters her kitchen followed by Michael. He is wearing a coat identical to the one he took off in Alison's flat*

It's kind of you to bring them all this way. You should have rung. I'd have collected them ... that would have saved you the trouble.

**Michael** It's no trouble. (*Immediately he spots his wicker basket on the floor. He does a double-take. He gives Lesley a sly look. He then addresses Alison although she is in her own living area*) She insisted on giving me a drink.

**Lesley** (*looking in a wall cupboard*) Oh damn ! We're not great drinkers ... it's only cooking sherry.

**Michael** It's all right ... don't bother. (*To Alison*) She offered me coffee instead.

**Lesley** Coffee then. You'll have a cup of coffee.

**Michael** (*to Alison*) I didn't really want one but (*nodding and smiling at Lesley*) I smiled and nodded. (*To Alison*) So she flicked on the electric kettle.

*Lesley does so*

The conversation had gone along quite nicely then all of a sudden there was this awkward pause.

*An awkward pause*

The two of us were frantically trying to think of something to say. She thought of something first.
**Lesley**  Do you drive?
**Michael**  Pardon?
**Lesley**  A car?
**Michael**  Er, no. Well I mean I do ... but I don't have one at the moment.
**Lesley**  So you came by bus then?

*He nods*

Then I must give you the fare.
**Michael**  There's no need.
**Alison**  It's not like you to refuse money.
**Lesley**  I can't let you be out of pocket.
**Michael**  (*to Alison*) I'm not tight. (*To Lesley*) It wasn't very much.
**Lesley**  (*getting her purse*) One pound twenty is one pound twenty.
**Michael**  OK. If you insist.
**Alison**  Are you going to go all round the mulberry?

*Lesley hands Michael the money then returns to making the coffee*

**Lesley**  Sugar?
**Michael**  One. (*Slight pause*) It's not a very good idea, you know.

*Lesley looks at him*

On the keys ... the address tag. I could be a thief.
**Alison**  You don't look like a thief.
**Michael**  (*to Alison*) Shut up!
**Lesley**  If you were, you'd hardly be returning them.
**Michael**  True ... but you get my point about key-tabs.
**Lesley**  (*thoughtfully*) Mmmmm.
**Michael**  (*to Alison*) She said something earlier that I found a bit odd. I thought it strange she should know the fare.
**Alison**  Did you ask her about it?

*He nods*

What did she say?

**Michael** She ignored me at first.
**Lesley** Milk?
**Michael** Please.

*She pours milk into the cups*

**Lesley** You said you found the keys near the bus station?
**Michael** Yes.
**Lesley** Well that's what it costs from there and back.
**Alison** There you are — a perfectly rational explanation.

*Andrew comes out of the bathroom and dials a number*

**Lesley** At least that's what I paid yesterday. I was visiting a friend and I must have lost them as she walked me there last night.
**Michael** (*to Alison*) Did you hear that? Did you hear what she said? I lost them, she said. It suddenly dawns on me that the keys don't belong to her brother at all — they're hers. (*To Lesley*) They're yours? The keys are yours?
**Lesley** Whose did you think?
**Michael** Your brother's, or husband's or something. It says Lesley, I thought ——
**Lesley** A lot of people do.
**Michael** (*to Alison*) I was gob-smacked. I mean I'd gone out all that way to get a look at this hunk that he upstairs cooked dinner for last night and I'm looking at her. She is Lesley.
**Alison** What did you do?
**Michael** I didn't know what to do. Luckily the telephone rang.

*The telephone rings*

**Lesley** Excuse me. (*Answering the telephone*) Hallo?
**Andrew** It's Andrew. Can you talk?
**Lesley** No, well yes.
**Andrew** Are you alone?
**Lesley** No, but it's all right. Look, I'm sorry about ringing earlier. I know you don't like being rung at work but I didn't know what else to do.
**Andrew** It's all right — listen, I've looked everywhere but I haven't found them.
**Lesley** It's all right — I've got them now.
**Michael** (*to Alison*) It's Andrew.
**Lesley** Someone found them near the bus station. He's brought them over. I'm giving him a cup of coffee — he's here now.

**Andrew**  Listen, I've got to talk to you.
**Lesley**  Now?
**Andrew**  Yes — can you take the call in another room?
**Lesley**  Not really, no.
**Andrew**  I'll have to ring you back then.
**Lesley**  I don't know. Perhaps it's better if I ring you.
**Andrew**  When?
**Lesley**  As soon as I can.
**Andrew**  Will you be long?
**Lesley**  I don't know.
**Andrew**  It's important.
**Lesley**  Maybe in an hour or so.
**Andrew**  Sooner.
**Lesley**  I'll try.
**Andrew**  OK. Bye.

*She replaces the receiver and looks rather uncomfortably at Michael*

**Lesley**  My friend.

*Michael nods disbelievingly*

   I rang her at work to ask if I'd left them at her house.

*Lesley turns away and pours coffee*

**Michael**  (*to Alison*) She's not a very good liar.
**Alison**  How did you know it was Andrew on the phone?
**Michael**  (*to Alison*) I asked her.
**Lesley**  Biscuit?
**Michael**  Look, ummm, I'm afraid I lied to you.
**Lesley**  What?
**Michael**  I don't feel bad about it because you lied to me too.
**Lesley**  I don't know what you're talking about.
**Michael**  I didn't find the keys near the bus station. I found them down the
   side of a bed-settee at 23b Pontcana Street.
**Lesley**  How do you know that address?
**Michael**  I live there.
**Lesley**  (*after a slight pause*) You know Andrew?
**Michael**  Oh yes.
**Lesley**  You live there with him? I mean you're his flat-mate or something?
**Michael**  No, he's mine. It's my flat. (*Slight pause*) You look surprised. He's
   never mentioned me?

**Lesley** (*in a mild state of shock*) No.

**Michael** No, he never mentioned you either. Was it him on the telephone just now?

*She nods. He gets up*

You won't mind if I don't have the coffee. I'd better get my bus back.

**Lesley** (*suspiciously*) Why did you come here?

**Michael** Curiosity, I suppose. I thought you were a man.

**Lesley** What does that mean?

**Michael** It means I thought Andrew had dinner with a fella last night.

**Lesley** Would it have made any difference to you if he had?

*He shrugs his shoulders*

Why hasn't he mentioned you?

**Michael** You'd better ask him that.

**Lesley** He definitely gave me the impression he lived alone. Why would he do that?

**Michael** Maybe he wanted to block any ideas you might have had about moving in.

**Lesley** (*snapping*) I had no intention of moving in !

**Michael** I only said maybe. (*To Alison*) Oooh, touched a nerve there, didn't I?

**Alison** The relationship sounds a bit scratchy to me.

**Michael** We'd both run out of things to say by this time.

**Alison** So what happened next?

**Michael** Bombshell number two. Someone shouted from the hall.

**Tom** (*off*) I'm off.

**Lesley** (*panicking*) It's my husband.

**Michael** And there he was standing at the door.

**Alison** And he's heard her.

**Michael** No.

**Alison** Where's this bombshell?

**Michael** Guess — guess who is standing in the doorway?

*Tom stands in the in the doorway*

**Tom** Is there anything else you want while I'm out? I don't fancy making the trip ... (*seeing Michael*) twice.

**Lesley** I thought you'd already gone.

**Michael** Hallo Tom.

**Alison** (*throwing her now empty plate on to the floor in amazement*) Tom?

**Lesley** You two know each other?

**Michael** Yes.

**Tom** (*jumping in*) From school.

**Alison** (*screaming*) Bloody liar!

**Tom** Michael's a lab technician in the science block — aren't you?

**Alison** (*to Michael*) What did you say?

**Michael** (*suiting the action to the words*) I just smiled and nodded my head slightly.

**Lesley** (*to Tom*) He found my keys. I lost them — I didn't tell you, I knew you'd make a fuss. (*To Michael*) You were just going, weren't you?

**Michael** (*to Alison*) She's giving me the elbow.

**Tom** (*eagerly*) Let me show you to the door.

**Michael** (*to Alison*) They're both glad to see the back of me.

**Lesley** It's all right — I'll go.

**Tom** (*insisting*) No no — I'll do it.

**Michael** (*to Alison*) They're each hoping to have a private word.

*He looks at each of them with a smile. They are standing either side of him*

Right then. I'm off.

*He goes*

*Tom and Lesley give each other a rather strained smile*

*Tom follows Michael*

*Lesley stays but tries to listen from the doorway*

(*Off*) He kept me at the door for a while making chit chat about this and that. It was pretty obvious he wanted to ask me if I'd mentioned you in any way, but he just couldn't come out with it. I couldn't bear to see him suffer any longer so I put him out of his misery and told him he had nothing to worry about on that score. Relieved as he undoubtedly was to hear it, I had the distinct impression he didn't absolutely believe me.

*Lesley dials a number*

*Michael comes in from the kitchen, (minus the coat) carrying a plate of scampi*

It's a fact of life though, isn't it? You tell someone something you know they want to hear, and the minute you tell them they suspect it.

**Alison** Scampi all right?
**Michael** I think so, yes.

*Alison and Michael both go off into the kitchen*

*The telephone rings in Michael's flat*

*Andrew comes out to answer it*

**Andrew** (*into the phone*) Yes.
**Lesley** I can't stay long, Tom's only gone to the door.
**Andrew** Oh ... right ... well ... I've just arranged a week off. (*Pause*) Are you still there?
**Lesley** Yes.
**Andrew** Oh good. As from today I've got a week off.
**Lesley** (*after a slight pause*) Yes. (*Slight pause*) You're going to have to hurry, Tom will be back any minute.
**Andrew** I've bought two tickets — airplane tickets. I've bought two seats on a night flight to Spain. Flying ten o'clock tonight. Coming?
**Lesley** You're not serious?
**Andrew** Don't you fancy it?
**Lesley** (*raising her voice*) How the hell can I go to Spain in my situation?
**Andrew** Don't shout — Tom, remember? Look, it's because of your situation I think we should go.
**Lesley** Andrew, I haven't the faintest idea what's going to happen to me. I still don't know what I'm going to do — but I know one thing: as much as I'd love to hop on a plane and fly off with you somewhere, I just can't do it with the way things are.
**Andrew** Don't you understand? There'll never be a better time to go than now.
**Lesley** If I go away with you tonight, what will happen this time next week when the holiday is over? What will I have to come back to?
**Andrew** Your situation won't be any worse than it is now.
**Lesley** At least for the time being I've still got a roof over my head.
**Andrew** Yeah but for how long? A week away will give you time to think.
**Lesley** It'll give me a lot more time than I want.
**Andrew** Look at it this way — it's only a matter of time before the shit hits the fan. The only choice you've got is the way in which it hits it.
**Lesley** What happened to the weekend away seeing a friend?
**Andrew** Sounded good in theory but I don't think you'll be able to pull it off.
**Lesley** (*after a slight pause*) Are you suggesting I keep the baby?
**Andrew** No, no, I'm not suggesting anything ... well I am. I'm suggesting you leave everything for a week. Put it on ice. If you're going to face the

music anyway, give yourself time to decide how you want to dance —
know what I mean? The way I see it is like this: you can either confront Tom
with it now and face the consequences, or you can have a wonderful week
away with me and face him when you come back. Now putting myself in
your position I know what I'd choose. Better to have something out of it.
What do you say?

**Lesley** (*after a slight pause*) I think you're a bastard — that's what I say.

**Andrew** What?

**Lesley** There are men in your position who would be offering someone like
me a hell of a lot more than a week in Spain.

**Andrew** But I can't go for a fortnight.

**Lesley** Look, I think I'd better stay and sort out my problem, because that's
what it is — my problem.

**Andrew** I've bought two tickets.

**Lesley** Take your flat-mate.

**Andrew** (*after a slight pause*) Who?

**Lesley** The one who shares with you.

**Andrew** How do you know about Michael?

**Lesley** Ask him when you see him.

**Andrew** You've made up your mind then?

*She doesn't answer*

You're sure you won't come?

*Slight pause*

**Lesley** (*quietly*) Positive.

*Slight pause*

**Andrew** Right, well I'll see you when I get back then.

**Lesley** No, no I don't think so.

**Andrew** Oh come on, don't be like that.

**Lesley** You're incredible, you know that? (*She hangs up*)

*Andrew goes off into Michael's bedroom*

*Lesley moves into the middle of the kitchen. She looks pensive*

*Tom comes to the kitchen doorway looking the same way*

*They suddenly become aware of each other. A pause. Tom's mother calls
from another room*

*Tom leaves immediately*

*Lesley sits at the table with her head in her hands*

*Michael and Alison come out of the kitchen and go into the bedroom area*

**Michael** Well, did that little tit-bit make you feel any better?
**Alison** It doesn't really change anything.
**Michael** Of course it does — at least you know his wife is messing about as well. That could change a lot.
**Alison** The fact that I know isn't going to change anything. It's if and when Tom knows that's when things might alter.
**Michael** Tom doesn't know. It was obvious from his reaction. (*He has an idea*) Hey, maybe I should tell him. I bet if he knew he'd be back here like a shot. (*He makes up his mind*) Yes, I'm going to tell him.
**Alison** Oh no you're not.
**Michael** What's the matter with you — it's what you want, isn't it?
**Alison** It may be what I want, but I don't want him just because he doesn't want his wife. I want him because he wants me. Promise you won't do anything to interfere — you won't ring him without me knowing or tell him anything, will you?
**Michael** What does it matter why he wants you as long as he does?
**Alison** It matters to me. Promise?
**Michael** It's the old pride again, isn't it? Rearing its ugly head.
**Alison** I want him, more than I want anything — but on my terms.
**Michael** Compromise.
**Alison** I've been compromising for years.
**Michael** So what's one more time?

*She shakes her head*

So you mean to tell me if Tom walked in here now and told you he wanted to make it up to you because he found out that his wife was having an affair, you'd show him the door?
**Alison** Yes.
**Michael** What more would you want from him?
**Alison** If he came here today I'd want him to tell me that he'd made a terrible mistake last night and that he'd changed his mind, not because of his wife's affair but because he wanted to live the rest of his life with me. Don't you see? It's important to me that the reason be the right one. You do see, don't you?
**Michael** (*after a slight pause*) Of course I do. It's just that if I were in your shoes, I'd rather have him for the wrong reason than not have him at all.

**Alison** If he doesn't come back — and I don't think he will — it means he's been having me for the wrong reason.

**Michael** No it doesn't. But if that's true then it shouldn't hurt.

**Alison** It doesn't. It just stings a bit.

**Michael** That's what having a relationship with an attached person is all about, stings and knocks. I've told you what to do about those. If I were you I'd go out. Don't stay in licking your wounds — see a movie.

**Alison** What if he came while I was out?

**Michael** Then he'll call again. Better for you if you were out. You don't want to let him think you're sitting here waiting for him.

**Alison** Come with me then. I haven't been to the cinema for years.

**Michael** Really? They're talking now, did you know?

*They both laugh*

**Alison** Oh very funny.

**Michael** Yeah, of course I'll come.

*Alison smiles. Slight pause*

**Alison** You'd better go up and see Andrew. Maybe he'd like you to see a film tonight.

**Michael** I wish. I'll see you later — about sevenish.

*Michael goes to his flat*

*Alison goes into the bathroom. As Michael goes into his flat, Andrew comes out of the bedroom carrying a small suitcase, some clothes and a pair of trainers. He is extremely happy. As he flings the open case down on the sofa he sings rather forcefully, "We're All Going on a Summer Holiday"*

**Michael** What's going on?

**Andrew** I've been looking for you — where have you been?

**Michael** I had to go out. What's with the suitcase?

**Andrew** It's all right, I'm not leaving. Well, not for good, anyway.

**Michael** Where are you going?

**Andrew** (*stopping packing to recite*) "Where the sea is as clear as a crystal spring — and the sun is as" ... I've forgotten the rest. I'm off to Spain for a week.

**Michael** Spain?

**Andrew** Eight days and seven glorious nights. It was a spur of the moment thing. There I was at work handing out plane tickets for every conceivable destination and I suddenly thought: I've had enough of this, when is it

going to be my turn? Now, I thought. Now is my turn. I got on the blower
and booked two night flights.

**Michael** Two?

**Andrew** A holiday's no fun on your own. Got a passport?

**Michael** What?

**Andrew** A passport?

**Michael** (*after a slight pause*) Er — yes.

**Andrew** Up to date?

**Michael** I think so.

**Andrew** Fancy coming then?

**Michael** Are you serious? I mean it's not some kind of a joke, is it?

**Andrew** (*pointing*) Tickets are over there. Fly ten o'clock tonight.

*Michael goes and picks the tickets up*

They're only a hundred and twenty quid apiece, flight only. No problem
with accommodation — I'll sort something out when we get there.

**Michael** (*smiling*) I don't believe it.

**Andrew** Well, what do you say — yes or no?

**Michael** Why me?

**Andrew** You're my flat-mate, aren't you? You're the one who's been
dropping hints right, left and centre about a holiday.

**Michael** Wouldn't you prefer to take Lesley?

**Andrew** (*after a slight pause*) Ah yes. I meant to ask you about her.

**Michael** I found the keys, didn't I. Curiosity got the better of me and I took
them back to her. Why are you asking me and not her? Or have you asked
her?

**Andrew** Look — things are a bit ... (*he shakes his hand*) with Lesley at the
moment. I need to get away. Need some distance between us. It's a bit
messy up here right now. (*He touches his head*) All sixes and sevens, you
know? (*Slight pause*) So, what's it to be?

**Michael** So you bought the tickets for me and you?

**Andrew** Of course I did. (*Slight pause*) You don't think I'd put out that kind
of money if I wasn't pretty sure you'd be interested. Hey, listen — if the
money's a problem ——

**Michael** No, no — there's no problem. I've got the money, I've got a cheque.
(*He goes to get his cheque book*) A hundred and twenty pounds you said?

**Andrew** You don't have to give it to me now.

**Michael** Yes, I want to. (*He writes a cheque*)

*Alison comes out of bathroom wearing a dressing-gown. She sits in the
bedroom and begins to put on make-up*

**Andrew** I'm not going to take all these. Just a couple of shorts and a few tops should be all right. How are you off for tops? There's one or two here if you want them.

**Michael** We're travelling light then, are we?

**Andrew** I'm not even going to take a suitcase — just throw a couple of things in my bag. (*He quickly puts the suitcase just inside the bedroom door*)

**Michael** Currency?

**Andrew** Exchange at the airport.

**Michael** How much are you taking?

**Andrew** (*packing some things into his sports bag*) Two hundred should be enough. Have you got that?

**Michael** Yeah, I've got that. (*He hands Andrew a cheque*) I don't believe this. One minute I'm going to the cinema with Alison and the next I'm off to Spain with you.

**Andrew** And who said life sucks, eh?

**Michael** I didn't.

**Andrew** Your passport — better get it — make sure it's in order.

**Michael** I can't remember when I saw it last.

*Michael goes into the bedroom. Andrew goes into the bathroom*

*Tom comes into his kitchen. He stands near the table where Lesley is sitting. There is a pause.*

**Tom** Les?

*Lesley looks up*

**Lesley** I thought you'd gone out.

**Tom** What is it? What's wrong.

**Lesley** Just leave me alone. I'll talk when I'm ready.

**Tom** So there is something. (*Slight pause*) It's me, isn't it?

**Lesley** I don't blame you any more than I blame myself.

**Tom** We can fix anything if we both want to.

**Lesley** I don't know that I want to.

**Tom** Is it that serious?

*She doesn't answer*

Talk to me. I'm sure we can sort this out.

**Lesley** Not this time, Tom. It's a mess, it's all a mess. (*She quietly begins to cry*)

*He touches her*

No don't ...
**Tom** Look, whatever it is we can get through it. We can get through anything
... you and me.
**Lesley** Even when there's someone else involved.

*There is a pause*

**Tom** (*thinking she means his affair*) Look ——
**Lesley** Don't say anything. Just sit down.

*He does*

Are you happy, Tom? I don't mean reasonably content — I mean happy.
**Tom** I thought I was.
**Lesley** I don't think you've been happy for a long time.
**Tom** What is happy, anyway? It's a mood. Something you experience every
now and then if you're lucky. It doesn't last — it's not meant to. Happy is
something you might be for short periods of time. (*Slight pause*) And there
have been times, haven't there?
**Lesley** But not for a long time.

*Michael comes out of his bedroom and begins to look for his passport in
a cupboard*

**Michael** I thought it might have been in my bedside cabinet.
**Lesley** Look, Tom — this isn't easy for me.
**Tom** I don't want to lose you.
**Lesley** There's someone else!
**Tom** All right but ——
**Lesley** I've been seeing someone else.

*Tom looks at her in total disbelief. He almost slumps down into a chair*

(*Finally*) Aren't you going to say something? Who is he? Is it serious? How
long has it been going on?

*A pause*

(*Exploding*) Ask something, for Christ sake!

*Another pause*

He's younger than me — he's twenty-nine. (*Slight pause*) His name's Andrew — I've been seeing him for three months. (*Slight pause*) He's asked me to go away with him.

*Tom still doesn't say anything*

Did you hear what I said? (*Slight pause*) He wants me to go away with him.
**Tom** (*after a slight pause*) Do you (*trying to find the right word*) care for him? I mean — do you, love him?
**Lesley** I don't know. (*Slight pause; correcting herself*) Yes. Yes, I do.

*He looks wrecked*

Tom, I know I'm hurting you but I'm hurting too.
**Tom** (*a very large sigh*) Oh Jesus.
**Lesley** And I'm pregnant.

*Michael finds his passport*

**Michael** (*shouting*) Got it!
**Tom** (*screaming*) You what? (*He raises his arm and hits Lesley in the face very forcefully*)

*Lesley is pushed towards the kitchen worktops. Tom goes after her and takes her by the arm and shakes her — this is followed by another blow across the face. Lesley loses her balance and falls to the floor, dragging him with her. This whole scene is done in slow motion and the slaps are obviously mimed. There should be some sort of sound and lighting effect here too — anything to help create the dramatic effect of the scene. The sound effect stops and immediately both Lesley and Tom freeze. They keep their position for some time*

**Michael** (*examining his passport*) Shit! What's the date today?

*Andrew comes out of the bathroom*

**Andrew** The thirtieth.
**Michael** When do we get back?
**Andrew** The sixth.
**Michael** That's when it's up. The sixth of June.
**Andrew** Well you're all right then.
**Michael** Are you sure? They will allow me back on the expiry date? Knowing my luck they'll detain me or something.

**Andrew** It is not out of date until the seventh.

**Michael** What if there are delays? What if there's a twelve hour delay and we're not back until the seventh?

**Andrew** Then it's their fault not yours.

**Michael** I wouldn't like to explain that to the Spaniards.

**Andrew** If it bothers you that much go and get another one. You'll just catch the Post Office. Mind you, it'll cost you over a tenner.

**Michael** (*after a slight pause*) I don't know what to do. What do you think?

**Andrew** I think — I know it's all right.

**Michael** I won't then. If you think it's all right then I won't bother.

**Andrew** You don't have to take my word for it.

**Michael** What resort are we going to?

**Andrew** I haven't booked accommodation remember? We can stay anywhere we like.

**Michael** Fancy a trip to Barcelona?

**Andrew** I don't know that I'll have time for trips. I want to spend most of the time on the beach working on a really good tan. Not easy in seven days. Now pack.

*They look at each other and share something. They are both smiling*

*Michael goes off into his bedroom*

*Andrew sits on the sofa and browses through the holiday brochure*

*Tom and Lesley have kept the same position. Pause*

**Tom** What do you want?

**Lesley** To be left alone.

**Tom** (*screaming*) It can't be my baby, can it?

**Lesley** (*screaming*) No! (*Slight pause. Quieter*) What do you want me to do?

**Tom** I don't think I want you to leave.

**Lesley** You don't think?

**Tom** (*raising his voice*) I'm mixed up too. (*Slight pause*) It's time we need. All right, not together — alone, and not with him.

**Lesley** (*shouting*) You've never hit me before. Is that why you did it? Because I was stupid enough to get pregnant?

*He doesn't answer her*

**Tom** (*trying to calm her*) You said you loved him. Does he feel the same? Yes, of course he does or he wouldn't be wanting to take you away.

**Lesley** (*turning away; crying*) You're wrong ... you're wrong. Oh he wants

me to go away with him, yes ... (*She laughs ironically*) But only for a week!
He's not offering me a future.

**Tom** (*stunned*) And you are considering this?

**Lesley** You've forgotten what it's like, haven't you?

**Tom** What?

**Lesley** At the beginning. There were times when there was nothing we
wouldn't give up just to sleep together.

**Tom** (*shouting*) I offered you everything.

**Lesley** If I wasn't pregnant would you have offered to marry me?

**Tom** Probably. Oh not when we did perhaps but the following year maybe.
(*Raising his voice*) The fact of the matter is when did you get pregnant, I
offered you a damn sight more than seven days away somewhere.

**Lesley** (*shouting*) Would you be more sympathetic if he offered to take me
on a three week cruise?

*There is a slight pause. Mother calls from another room. They stare at each
other*

*Tom leaves the kitchen*

*After he has gone she grimaces. There is another sound effect similar to the
one heard earlier. She puts her hand down to her lower stomach. She gives
the impression she is more uncomfortable than she is in pain. She realizes
something and hurriedly leaves the kitchen. Immediately she disappears the
sound stops*

*Michael comes out of the bedroom*

**Michael** What time are we leaving?

**Andrew** We've got a while yet. Say we leave here about eight. That'll give
us time to get the bus to the airport.

**Michael** I'm going down to tell Alison.

*He taps her radiator. She doesn't hear it, she is still in her bedroom*

I promised I'd go to the cinema.

**Andrew** Oh well if you'd rather ...

**Michael** You've got to be joking.

**Andrew** Take a key. I'm going to shower.

*Michael leaves the flat to go to Alison's*

*Andrew goes off into the bathroom*

**Michael** Oh good — you haven't got ready yet.

**Alison** No but ——

**Michael** Look, Al ... I'm going to have to let you down. But when I tell you why you won't mind. I'm off to Spain. With Andrew.

**Alison** That's wonderful.

**Michael** When he said he wanted me and it was urgent he wasn't kidding. We're flying at ten o'clock tonight. Can you believe it?

**Alison** (*after a slight pause*) I don't want to put ice on the fire, but are you sure you've got it right? I'm thinking about last night and the meal and everything.

**Michael** I've paid for my ticket. I've almost finished packing.

**Alison** I just don't want you to get hurt.

**Michael** It's all arranged. We're going to have a terrific time. (*Slight pause*) I know it's a rotten time for you but I'd like you to be pleased for me.

**Alison** I am.

**Michael** What will you do — will you go anyway? To the cinema?

**Alison** No, I'm not going to bother. I think I'll stay in and commit suicide.

*He looks at her*

Don't worry, I was only kidding.

**Michael** I should think so. He's not worth it. Nobody is.

**Alison** Not even Andrew?

**Michael** Certainly not Andrew. (*Slight pause*) You haven't heard from Tom then? He hasn't rung or anything?

*She shakes her head*

Do you want to make a bet with me?

*She doesn't answer*

I'll bet you lunch a week tomorrow — that's the day we get back — that Tom will be here talking to you before Monday.

**Alison** (*smiling*) I think you're going to owe me. Stay here.

*She goes into the kitchen*

*Michael sits on the bed*

*Lesley comes into her kitchen wearing a bathrobe*

**Lesley** (*to the audience*) When Tom left I thought he went in to see his mother, but he went out. He'll be back, of course. I don't know when but he'll be back. He's got to, hasn't he? (*Slight pause*) With me it's different. I could walk out of the door now and never come back.

*A pause as she looks at the audience. Then she goes to the telephone and dials. The phone in Michael's flat rings*

*Andrew comes out of the bathroom to answer it. He is wearing a bathrobe*

**Andrew** Hallo?
**Lesley** It's me.
**Andrew** Hi. Everything all right?
**Lesley** No. Well, yes. (*Pause*) I mean, the balloon's gone up here.
**Andrew** You've told him then.
**Lesley** Yes.
**Andrew** How did it go?
**Lesley** Not as I expected. It's all a bit of a mess — but that's not why I called. I was just calling to let you know that everything is all right with me. I mean ... I mean I'm not pregnant.
**Andrew** You're not? That's wonderful. (*Slight pause*) Isn't it wonderful?
**Lesley** Yes, it's wonderful. It's tremendous.
**Andrew** What happened?
**Lesley** Well I had my period, that's what happened.
**Andrew** What — just like that?
**Lesley** No, not just like that. Tom got violent and threw me around a bit. It must have done something.
**Andrew** Well it's good news anyway, eh?

*Pause*

**Lesley** I've been thinking. Things are obviously different now — a different situation to a couple of hours ago ...

*Alison comes out of the kitchen with a bottle of wine and two glasses*

**Alison** (*entering; overlapping Lesley*) I bought this for after dinner last night but he didn't stay long enough to drink it. Open it.

*Lesley and Andrew continue their conversation in mime*

**Michael** Why don't you keep it? He will be back.
**Alison** Open it. (*A thought strikes her*) Hey, you haven't been doing anything, have you?

*He doesn't understand*

You sound so sure about Tom. You promised you wouldn't interfere.
**Michael** I haven't. I swear I haven't.

*She believes him*

I just know he won't leave it as it is.

*He opens the wine and pours it. She hands him a glass*

**Alison** (*toasting*) To you and Andy.

*Michael raises his glass and they drink. Lesley and Andrew finish their conversation and hang up*

*Beaming with success, Andrew shakes his fists and rushes off back into the bathroom*

**Alison** Where are you staying?
**Michael** He's going to arrange accommodation when we get there. Maybe for the first night we'll bunk down on the beach somewhere.
**Alison** Romantic.

*Michael smiles wickedly*

Tom and I never once went away.
**Michael** Did he used to go away with Lesley?
**Alison** Nowhere really far. She wouldn't fly and couldn't go by coach because of her ankles.

*He looks at her*

They swell apparently.

*They both laugh. Slight pause*

Has there been anyone else besides Tom?
**Alison** I had a fling before I met him but nothing serious. I've never really seen myself without him.

*Tom enters L. He walks straight into Alison's flat*

*She continues talking. Both she and Michael are unaware for a moment that he has entered the room*

That's going to be the difficult part. Work is the answer — it usually is.

*Michael sees Tom over Alison's shoulder. He lets her continue*

Of course it would have to happen now when I've got a bloody week off. (*Looking at Michael*) What's the matter?
**Michael** I think you owe me lunch.

*She doesn't understand. Michael nods for her to turn around. She does and sees Tom*

**Tom** Celebrating?
**Alison** &#125; (*together*) &#123; Yes, actually.
**Michael** &#125;            &#123; Not really.
**Alison** I didn't hear you come in.
**Tom** Obviously.

*There is an awkward pause*

**Michael** Well, I'm off.
**Alison** You don't have to go.
**Michael** Yes I do. I've still got a couple of things to pack.
**Tom** Off somewhere?

*Michael nods and smiles*

**Michael** (*to Alison*) I won't call in before I leave.
**Alison** Have a great time.

*They give each other a peck*

Take the bottle with you. Finish it upstairs.

*Michael takes the bottle and leaves*

*Slight pause*

**Tom** (*indicating her make-up*) Going out?
**Alison** Yes. (*Slight pause*) Actually. (*She takes her wine and goes into the bedroom to finish her make-up and to dress*)

*Left alone, Tom looks rather uncomfortable. After a moment he sits*

*Michael enters his flat*

**Michael** (*at the bathroom door, calling*) Are you going to be long in there?
**Alison** (*replying to Tom*) As long as it takes.
**Tom** I've got to talk to you.
**Michael** What about?

*Andrew comes out of the bathroom*

**Andrew** Something's come up.
**Michael** What is it? (*Slight pause*) It's still on, is it?
**Andrew** No, it isn't.
**Michael** You're joking. You've got to be joking.
**Andrew** Sorry.
**Michael** Has the flight been cancelled or what?
**Andrew** No, no it's still on — but not for us. Well not for you. (*Slight pause*) Change of plan. You've got to understand.
**Michael** I've got a feeling I'm not going to.
**Andrew** I can't go with you.
**Michael** Oh, so you're not going either?
**Andrew** Yes — I am — but not with you.
**Michael** Look, what's going on? One minute I'm going to Spain with you — I nip downstairs for a quarter of an hour — and when I get back it's all off.
**Andrew** I've had a phone call. I can't go into it — it's personal.
**Michael** (*shouting*) Personal? I don't care how personal it is — you owe me an explanation.
**Andrew** Things have happened.
**Michael** Is it Lesley? (*Slight pause*) It is, isn't it?
**Andrew** I wish it didn't have to happen.
**Michael** What do you think I am?
**Andrew** Don't get all worked up.
**Michael** You really piss me off, you know that? I mean apart from anything else, you didn't even ask. No decent explanation — no apology, just "something's come up and it's off". Without any conscience — nothing.
**Andrew** (*sitting on the sofa*) I do feel terrible about it.
**Michael** You don't feel terrible about anything — you never have.
**Andrew** It's only a holiday.
**Michael** It might only have been a holiday to you, but it was going to mean a hell of a lot more to me.
**Andrew** Well it wouldn't have been. Better to be disappointed here than there.

**Michael** You can cut that crap with me. I haven't got you wrong.

**Andrew** I'm not what you think. I'm straight, Michael.

**Michael** How can you say that?

**Andrew** I know what I am.

**Michael** You said earlier you needed to get away from Lesley. Needed distance between you. You said you were all confused — or words to that effect.

**Andrew** I was — I still am about my feelings towards her. But I know exactly where I am with you.

**Michael** Why are you doing this? OK, so you'd rather go to Spain with Lesley than with me — but that doesn't make you straight.

**Andrew** Going with you doesn't make me gay.

**Michael** You slept with me. You've ——

**Andrew** One toss doesn't make a salad, pal.

**Michael** No, and it doesn't make a lot of sense, either. You can't have done the things we've done and be straight.

**Andrew** You think I did those things for me?

**Michael** You're not trying to say it was all one sided?

**Andrew** I got nothing out of it.

**Michael** You bastard.

**Andrew** I knew what you were when I came here.

**Michael** Too right you did. You knew exactly what I was and you used it.

**Andrew** Yeah, I won't deny that.

**Michael** That's big of you.

**Andrew** That night we spent together, it should never have happened.

**Michael** But it did. And I'll tell you something else. You knew it would happen at some point.

**Andrew** I did it for you.

**Michael** Why didn't it seem like that at the time?

**Andrew** What would be the point of doing it if I let you suspect it wasn't mutual?

**Michael** What would be the point of doing it and let me think it was? Friends don't do it, Andrew. And room-mates don't either.

**Andrew** It doesn't matter what you say.

**Michael** Are you running away? Because if you are you're not going to hide in Spain. You're not running away from me — you're running away from yourself — don't you see that? I don't want to corrupt you — God forbid — but I've never forced you to do anything — and straight people don't do what we did voluntarily.

**Andrew** I know why I did it.

**Michael** Then tell me. OK — let's assume that what I've just said is wrong. Do you really think that much of me as a friend?

**Andrew** (*after a slight pause*) Yes.

**Michael** Then why do you treat me like shit?

**Andrew** I don't. You only think I do because of how you feel about me.

**Michael** Oh, so you are aware of how I feel?

*He doesn't answer*

Answer me this. If you know how I feel about you, how can you bring someone to my flat? How can you ask me to go to Spain and then tell me you want my ticket for someone else? (*Slight pause*) I know what I feel for you isn't mutual — but I can live with that. (*Slight pause*) I don't know why you slept with me that night — but I suspect deep down you do. (*Slight pause*) I might not be that special person for you, Andrew, but at some point, somewhere, you're going to meet him — and when you do — Pow! And it won't matter if you're with Lesley or any other female. You see I think we've all got this ... door — inside somewhere. We all have one. Male and female. We don't know where it is but we guard it with our lives, because through that door is the secret to everything. Happiness, misery — (*Slight pause*) It's all very personal and we're very careful as to who we let in. For me — it's you. Now you might not want to go through this door, but it doesn't matter. The fact that I've given you the key gives you great power and makes you stronger than me. And because you're stronger and because you want it ... I know I'm going to end up giving you my ticket.

**Andrew** I have to go with Lesley.

**Michael** Won't you even think about what I've said?

**Andrew** A lot of what you say makes sense — but you don't understand me. Sometimes I don't understand myself. I don't want to be gay.

**Michael** Do you think I did?

**Andrew** I only ever did it the once.

**Michael** Maybe, but I bet you've thought about it more than that.

**Andrew** I think more about women.

**Michael** Then why did it happen with us?

**Andrew** Because I knew you wanted it to.

**Michael** And?

**Andrew** And I probably wanted to find out what it was like.

**Michael** And what was it like?

**Andrew** I don't want to talk about it.

**Michael** Can't handle it?

**Andrew** I can handle anything. (*Slight pause*) For me it was a sort of experiment, that's all. It didn't mean anything. I can't help it if it did to you.

**Michael** Oh please, don't spare my feelings.

**Andrew** What?

**Michael** No, go on.

**Andrew** Nothing more to say. End of story.

**Michael** You haven't told me what it was like for you.

*Andrew doesn't answer him*

Shall I tell you what I think? I think it was great for you — wonderful for you. I think it was so bloody tremendous it frightened the shit out of you.

**Andrew** (*shouting*) No !

**Michael** Then be honest and tell me differently.

**Andrew** You're pushing me and I don't want you to.

**Michael** I only want you to look at yourself.

**Andrew** You're confusing me.

**Michael** No, I'm trying to sort you out.

**Andrew** Just leave me alone, will you? I curse the day I came here.

**Michael** Why? Because I helped you find yourself?

**Andrew** You haven't helped me find fuck all.

**Michael** I've made you ask yourself a lot of questions though, haven't I? You shouldn't blame me if you don't like the answers.

**Andrew** (*angrily*) You're talking shit! You can say what you like but you're talking shit !

**Michael** Then what's the problem? If I am why are you so sensitive about it?

**Andrew** (*snapping*) OK, OK. So you're saying I'm bisexual. I did it once and you're saying I'm bisexual. I can still have a preference.

**Michael** Of course you can. But can you always stick by it?

**Andrew** Why shouldn't I?

**Michael** Why didn't you? (*Slight pause*) Look, I'm not the baddie here. I'm not trying to turn you into something you're not. I'm trying to help you.

**Andrew** And get your seat back to Spain.

**Michael** I haven't given it to you yet to want it back.

**Andrew** But you will — you said you would.

**Michael** Do you have any idea what you're asking me to do?

**Andrew** It's nothing to what you're asking me.

**Michael** I only want you to be yourself.

**Andrew** You want me to be the same as you and I can't — I can't. I hate gays.

**Michael** You don't hate me.

**Andrew** (*shouting*) I think you're disgusting.

**Michael** Don't say that.

**Andrew** You're no better than vermin.

**Michael** Andrew !

**Andrew** Scum of the earth. I'd hate to be like you. I hate everything about you.

*They are both shouting now*

**Michael** Everything?

**Andrew** You want to know what I felt that night? Sick. I felt sick!

**Michael** Then why didn't I see any? Why did you go through with it? Why did you carry on right to the end?

**Andrew** (*after a pause*) You're repulsive — you know that?

*He spits in Michael's face. A pause*

*Michael turns and runs out of the flat. He goes downstairs and races out of the building*

*Andrew, after a slight pause, sits on the sofa. His position should match exactly that as at the beginning of the play. He stays there, motionless*

*A slight pause*

**Alison** Are you still there, Tom?

**Tom** Yes, I'm still here.

**Alison** (*coming out from the bedroom fastening her earrings*) Twice in two days — what have I done to deserve it?

**Tom** I didn't want to leave things the way they were.

**Alison** You've more to say?

**Tom** Well, we didn't really say much last night.

**Alison** You said enough.

**Tom** (*after a slight pause*) I'm not sure why I'm here.

**Alison** Oh that's great.

**Tom** (*after a slight pause*) We've known each other a long time, Al. I think we both deserve better than we gave each other last night.

**Alison** So that's why you've come — to wrap it all up properly.

**Tom** Last night I didn't want to wrap it up at all.

**Alison** And today?

*Slight pause*

**Tom** Lesley's pregnant.

*Slight pause*

**Alison** Suddenly everything falls into place.

**Tom** It's not mine.

**Alison** Now I'm confused again.

**Tom** It's pretty straightforward: she's having a baby by someone else.

**Alison** Tom. Tom, last night ... last night I was wrong. I went about things the wrong way. I know I said I didn't want part of you, and on that score nothing has changed ... but I said those things because I wanted all of you. I still do.

**Tom** Things aren't the same anymore.

**Alison** Of course they're not — and if we're sensible we can turn them to our own advantage.

**Tom** There's still no future for us, Al.

**Alison** Don't say that. (*Slight pause*) You're hurt and upset. Let's leave it for now. I don't want to do that but maybe it's what's best for you. We don't have to make any decisions at the moment.

**Tom** I do.

**Alison** Yes of course you do as far as Lesley is concerned, but I was talking about us. I understand she's hurt you, Tom, but I'm still here for you. You can't blame me but I'm glad she's done this to you.

**Tom** She hasn't done anything to me I wouldn't have done to her in a similar situation. If men carried kids I've no doubt I'd have been pregnant the first three months you and I were together.

**Alison** (*annoyed*) It was the same for me. Why didn't it happen to me? I'll tell you why — because I didn't want to be pregnant.

**Tom** You're telling me Lesley did?

**Alison** No woman need get pregnant today, Tom. If she's having a baby nine times out of ten it's because she wants it — and if she wants it she obviously doesn't want you — and if she says she does you can stake your life it's because the other guy doesn't want her.

**Tom** No — that's not it at all. She's confused.

**Alison** Aren't we all.

**Tom** She doesn't know what she wants at the moment and neither do I.

**Alison** Let's have a cooling-off period.

**Tom** We've been cool for a long time.

**Alison** (*shouting*) No!

**Tom** It's true last night in bed ——

**Alison** That was nothing. I didn't mean what I said. I wasn't being honest with you. I lied. (*Getting upset*) Don't leave, Tom.

*Pause*

Please. (*Quietly*) Don't leave me?

**Tom** It would have been easier if this had happened ... I don't know ... five, six years ago. Everything was different then. (*Slight pause*) You're right — it's not the same anymore. We're not the same.

**Alison** (*shouting*) I haven't changed.

**Tom** (*shouting*) All right I have.

**Alison** You can't still want her?

**Tom** I don't know what I want ... only what I don't want.

**Alison** (*after a slight pause*) Me.

**Tom** I can't turn to you because Lesley doesn't want me. That wouldn't be fair.

**Alison** Oh we're talking fair now, are we?

**Tom** I couldn't do that to you.

**Alison** What you're doing to me is worse. If I'm prepared to take you on those terms then that's my decision. And I will, Tom. I'll take it anyway you want to dish it out only don't go.

**Tom** (*upset*) It's dead, Al — and if now's the time to be completely honest with each other we both know it and have known it for a long time. It's dead.

**Alison** (*shouting*) No!

**Tom** We just haven't got round to burying it, that's all.

**Alison** (*dragging him into the bedroom*) Come to bed.

**Tom** Don't do this.

**Alison** Come on — it'll be much better than the last time, I promise. (*She tries to undress him*)

**Tom** What are you doing?

**Alison** I want you.

**Tom** You're making a fool of yourself.

**Alison** It's not for the first time — anyway it doesn't matter anymore.

**Tom** (*struggling with her*) I don't want you to do this.

**Alison** (*trying to pull him down on to the bed*) Oh but you do, Tom. It's going to be wonderful. You're going to be wonderful.

*They freeze. Their position too should now match that of the start of the play*

> *To complete the picture, Lesley comes into her kitchen with her suitcase and the note she is about to leave on the door of the fridge. Immediately she is in position, Michael comes on* L. *He enters to the same music that is used in the opening scene. He takes up his position* C

**Michael** (*to the audience*) Well ... this is it. The point at which you all came in. (*Pause*) I wish I knew yesterday what I know today. (*He smiles almost to himself*) How many of us have said that in our time? (*Slight pause*) It's easy, isn't it — to be wise after the event — though some people never learn. Would I have done anything differently? I doubt it. I've always been a sucker for a pretty face. And there's a hell of a lot of us out there. (*Slight pause*) Anyway — I need to know — not just if I'm going to Spain — but how I'm going to come out of all this. (*Slight pause*) Time to find out.

*Michael goes up to his flat*

*Andrew comes out of the bedroom carrying a suitcase*

**Michael**  I was afraid you'd gone.
**Andrew**  Just going.

*Lesley puts the message on the door of the fridge and leaves her kitchen*

**Michael**  I thought you weren't taking a suitcase.
**Andrew**  I'm not. I'm dropping it off somewhere.
**Michael**  What do you mean?
**Andrew**  Well, I can't come back here, can I?
**Michael**  Of course you can.
**Andrew**  I'm going away with Lesley.
**Michael**  I don't care. Well I do care, of course I care, but it doesn't matter.
(*Slight pause*) Look, let's forget about it. It didn't happen, OK? Nothing
ever happened between us — it's gone — forgotten.
**Andrew**  (*after a slight pause*) No. I want out.

*Pause*

**Michael**  Where will you go?
**Andrew**  I don't know.
**Michael**  Stay until you do then.
**Andrew**  You'll never let me go.
**Michael**  Stay until you've sorted yourself out.
**Andrew**  (*shaking his head*) No.
**Michael**  What do you want from me? My airticket? You've got it. You want
me to accept you're going away with Lesley — I accept. If you want me
to be here when you get back, I'll be here.
**Andrew**  It's useless, you've got to see that.
**Michael**  I'll beg. I beg you please, don't do this to me.
**Andrew**  (*turning on him*) Hey, listen pal, I'm not doing anything. You're
doing all this yourself.
**Michael**  Jesus Christ, can't anyone reach you?
**Andrew**  At last you've got the message.
**Michael**  All right, don't stay until you've sorted yourself out — stay until
I've sorted myself out. (*Backing away and sitting in the armchair*) Do
something for me — do something for someone else for a change.
**Andrew**  Coming back here isn't going to help either of us.
**Michael**  It'll give me something to hang on to.
**Andrew**  Exactly.
**Michael**  Only long enough to get on top of all this. Please — I honestly don't
know what I might end up doing.

**Andrew** (*raising his voice*) Don't you threaten me.

**Michael** I'm not.

**Andrew** (*shouting*) You're trying to tell me that you might do something stupid.

**Michael** All right then, yes I might.

**Andrew** Do it then! You want to stick your head in the oven — there's fifty pence for the gas. (*He throws him a coin*)

**Michael** (*getting up*) You flatter yourself. You think I'd top myself for you? Nobody would do that. You're a bastard — and once a bastard always a bastard.

**Andrew** Time to go.

**Michael** Yeah, go on, piss off!

*Andrew gets his sports bag and suitcase*

**Andrew** Just one piece of advice before I go ——

**Michael** I don't want it.

**Andrew** Next time you advertise for someone to share — don't choose anyone so good looking. (*He throws the key down on the coffee table*) Well, that's it. I hope I'm not leaving anything behind.

**Michael** Only me. Bastard!

*Tom frees himself from Alison's grip and goes into the living area*

(*Taking the suitcase from Andrew and throwing it down the stairs*) I hope there's a ten hour delay! (*He does the same with the sports bag*) I hope it pisses down the entire week!

*Tom takes his key out of his pocket and leaves it on Alison's table*

*Andrew leaves*

**Michael** (*calling after him*) I hope your balls fester and drop off!

*Suddenly Andrew trips and falls down three or four steps*

*Michael goes into his flat. He is obviously very upset. He stands in the centre of his living-room with his back to the audience*

*Tom comes out of Alison's flat as Andrew falls down the stairs. Tom goes to him and helps him to his feet*

**Tom** Are you all right?

**Andrew**  (*in extreme pain*) He fucking wished this on me.
**Tom**  (*picking up Andrew's luggage*) Can you get up?
**Andrew**  I've twisted my ankle.
**Tom**  Try walking.

*Andrew gets up*

Here, wait a minute. (*He takes Andrew's arm and puts it around his neck*)
That's right, put your weight on me. I'll give you a hand to the door. Are
you going far? Can give you a lift.
**Andrew**  The airport.
**Tom**  (*after a slight pause*) Well, come on — I've got nothing better to do.

*Tom and Andrew freeze at the end of the corridor. Music begins to play:
Freddie Mercury and Monserrat Caballé singing "Barcelona"*

*Alison remains motionless on the bed but Michael is upset and begins to
move: in a small area at first but the more frustrated he becomes the larger
the area he covers. His emotion and frustration build to a peak and eventually
they break out and he starts to throw the cushions off the sofa and across the
room. When he has done that he tips the sofa over on to its front. Then he starts
in another part of the room slowly but surely wrecking it. He sweeps
everything off the top of the unit and does it with such force he ends up on the
floor in a heap of rubbish. He is still upset and is crying but very subtly his
sobs turn to laughter — the laughter goes on until he's quite hysterical. He
is holding something in his hand. He rolls over on to his back and thrusts his
hand into the air in time to Freddie Mercury singing "Barcelona". He has
the plane tickets. He carries on laughing as——*

*— the* CURTAIN *falls*

# FURNITURE AND PROPERTY LIST

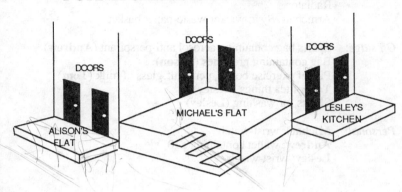

## ACT I
### SCENE 1

*On stage*:    LESLEY'S KITCHEN
Fridge. *In it*: yoghurt, milk
Kitchen units with worktops. *In cupboard*: bottle of shampoo,
   bowl of sugar. *On worktop*: electric kettle (practical)
Table. *On it*: plate with food, cutlery
Chairs
Washing machine. *In it*: washing
Linen basket
Pedal bin
Telephone on wall
Sink. *On it*: dishcloth
Suitcase and note (for **Lesley**)

ALISON'S LIVING-ROOM/BEDROOM
Sofa
Chairs
Table. *On it*: telephone
Radiator
Bed. *On it*: bedclothes
Dressing-table. *On it*: mirror, various make-up items, earrings

MICHAEL'S LIVING-ROOM
Sofa. *On it*: holiday brochure, cushions
Coffee table. *On it*: table lamp, telephone, small toffee hammer,
    stereo cassette player
Cupboard. *In it*: passport
Radiator
Armchair. *By it*: wicker waste-paper basket

*Off stage*:    Sports bag containing aerosol anti-perspirant (**Andrew**)
                Bag containing groceries (**Alison**)
                Pile of exercise books, pen, half-glass of milk (**Tom**)
                Tray of tea things (**Lesley**)
                Sheets for washing (**Lesley**)

*Personal*:     **Michael**: wrist-watch
                **Andrew**: wallet containing £10
                **Lesley**: wrist-watch

## SCENE 2

*Set*:          Squash kit and sports bag in **Lesley**'s kitchen

*Off stage*:    Towel (**Andrew**)
                Piece of paper, handbag containing various items including a
                    purse with coins and a handkerchief (**Lesley**)
                Bottle of wine, 2 glasses (**Andrew**)
                Botttle of wine, 2 glasses (**Alison**)
                Tray with dinner plates containing food, etc. (**Andrew**)
                Tray with dinner plates containing food, etc. (**Alison**)
                Bottle of wine (**Andrew**)

*Personal*:     **Andrew**: Goldspot spray
                **Alison**: Goldspot spray

## ACT II

*Set*:          Bunch of keys on sofa in **Michael**'s living-room
                Blankets in washing machine in **Lesley**'s kitchen

*Off stage*:    Plate of fried scampi (**Alison**)
                Plate of fried scampi (**Michael**)

Small suitcase, clothes, pairs of trainers (**Andrew**)
Bottle of wine, 2 glasses, corkscrew (**Alison**)

*Personal*:   **Andrew**: 2 airline tickets, coin, key
**Michael**: cheque book, pen
**Tom**: key

# LIGHTING PLOT

Practical fittings required: table lamp for **Michael's** living-room. Three interiors

ACT I, Scene 1. Evening

*To open*: Black-out

| | | |
|---|---|---|
| *Cue 1* | Music stops playing<br>*Bring up spot on **Michael** and low soft light on set* | (Page 1) |
| *Cue 2* | **Michael** turns to look at the three areas<br>*Slowly increase lighting overall* | (Page 1) |
| *Cue 3* | **Michael**: "I've got a terrible feeling he has."<br>*Change to flashing coloured circles of light overall* | (Page 2) |
| *Cue 4* | **Michael** switches on the table lamp<br>*Snap off flashing coloured lighting, snap on practical<br>in living-room and covering spot* | (Page 2) |
| *Cue 5* | **Andrew** rings the doorbell<br>*Increase lighting overall* | (Page 3) |
| *Cue 6* | **Michael**: "Shit!"<br>*Black-out* | (Page 16) |

ACT I, Scene 2. Evening

*To open*: Interior lighting in **Alison's** flat L and **Lesley's** kitchen R

| | | |
|---|---|---|
| *Cue 7* | **Alison**: "... the penny to finally drop."<br>*Concentrate lighting in tight circle on two areas* | (Page 17) |
| *Cue 8* | **Tom** exits<br>*Cross-fade to **Alison's** flat* | (Page 18) |

*Cue* 9     **Alison** goes into the kitchen        (Page 18)
                 *Bring up lighting on* **Michael'***s flat*

*Cue* 10    **Andrew** goes into the bathroom       (Page 19)
                 *Fade lighting on* **Michael'***s flat*

*Cue* 11    **Alison** switches off the light        (Page 20)
                 *Black-out; bring up spot* L

*Cue* 12    **Lesley** exits                    (Page 20)
                 *Cross-fade to general lighting on* **Alison'***s flat*

*Cue* 13    **Lesley** presses the correct bell      (Page 21)
                 *Bring up lighting in* **Michael'***s flat*

*Cue* 14    **Lesley** switches on the light        (Page 31)
                 *Snap on lighting in kitchen*

*Cue* 15    **Michael** puts out the light         (Page 34)
                 *Snap off lighting in* **Michael'***s flat*

*Cue* 16    **Alison** switches off her light        (Page 34)
                 *Snap off lighting in* **Alison'***s flat*

*Cue* 17    **Tom** switches off the light in the kitchen    (Page 34)
                 *Black-out*

## ACT II. Day

*To open*: Bright sunlight effect in **Lesley**'s kitchen; general lighting in **Michael**'s flat; dim lighting in **Alison**'s flat

*Cue* 18    **Michael** goes into the kitchen         (Page 35)
                 *Cross-fade to small coloured light in* **Alison**'*s flat*

*Cue* 19    **Alison**'s double runs into the bathroom    (Page 37)
                 *Revert to opening lighting*

*Cue* 20    **Lesley**: " ... there was a rather large desk."    (Page 38)
                 *Reduce to spot on* **Lesley**

*Cue* 21    **Lesley:** " ... been able to do that."                    (Page 38)
            *Revert to opening lighting*

*Cue* 22    **Tom** hits **Lesley**                                     (Page 58)
            *Lighting change; flashing coloured lights or similar*
               *effect*

*Cue* 23    **Tom** and **Lesley** freeze                              (Page 58)
            *Revert to opening lighting*

# EFFECTS PLOT

## ACT I

*Cue* 1    When the CURTAIN rises                              (Page 1)
       *Music*

*Cue* 2    When the cast is in position                        (Page 1)
       *Cut music*

*Cue* 3    **Michael**: "I've got a terrible feeling he has."   (Page 2)
       *Abba recording of "Take a Chance on Me"*

*Cue* 4    **Michael** switches on the table lamp              (Page 2)
       *Cut music*

*Cue* 5    **Michael** presses the button on his stereo cassette  (Page 2)
       *Recording of female opera singer*

*Cue* 6    **Michael**: " ... for seven nights.'"              (Page 2)
       *Cut music*

*Cue* 7    **Michael**: "I could just about manage that."      (Page 2)
       *Sound of running water*

| | | |
|---|---|---|
| *Cue* 8 | **Michael:** "Hear it?"<br>*Water sound stops* | (Page 2) |
| *Cue* 9 | **Andrew** rings **Michael's** doorbell<br>*Doorbell* | (Page 3) |
| *Cue* 10 | **Alison:** " ... a second time on the telephone."<br>**Alison's** *telephone* | (Page 7) |
| *Cue* 11 | **Lesley** puts sheets in the washing machine<br>**Lesley's** *telephone* | (Page 10) |
| *Cue* 12 | **Andrew** dials. Quick pause<br>**Lesley's** *telephone* | (Page 12) |
| *Cue* 13 | **Tom** dials a number. Quick pause<br>**Alison's** *telephone* | (Page 13) |
| *Cue* 14 | **Tom** leaves the kitchen<br>**Lesley's** *telephone* | (Page 15) |
| *Cue* 15 | **Alison:** "... the penny to finally drop."<br>*Music* | (Page 17) |
| *Cue* 16 | **Andrew:** "All in a day's living, right?"<br>**Michael's** *telephone* | (Page 19) |
| *Cue* 17 | **Tom** kisses **Alison**<br>*Music* | (Page 20) |
| *Cue* 18 | The Lights fade to Black-out<br>*Cut music* | (Page 20) |
| *Cue* 19 | **Alison:** " ... 'Hurry up, for Christ's sake'."<br>**Alison's** *doorbell* | (Page 21) |
| *Cue* 20 | **Lesley** presses the correct doorbell<br>**Michael's** *doorbell* | (Page 21) |
| *Cue* 21 | **Alison:** "You're going to have to make a choice."<br>*Uncomfortable sound effect* | (Page 27) |
| *Cue* 22 | **Lesley** grabs a quiet moment to herself<br>*Door slam* | (Page 31) |

*Cue* 36   **Lesley** dials. Pause                                    (Page 62)
           **Michael'**s *telephone*

*Cue* 37   **Michael** comes on L                                    (Page 71)
           *Music as at opening to Act I*

*Cue* 38   **Tom** and **Andrew** freeze                             (Page 74)
           *Recording of "Barcelona" by Freddie Mercury and*
           *Monserrat Caballé*

MADE AND PRINTED IN GREAT BRITAIN BY
LATIMER TREND & COMPANY LTD PLYMOUTH

MADE IN ENGLAND